The Poetry Review

The Poetry Society, 22 Betterton Street, London WC2H 9BX

The Poetry Review

The Poetry Society, 22 Betterton Street, London WC2H 9BX
Tel: +44 (0)20 7420 9880 • Fax: +44 (0)20 7240 4818
Email: poetryreview@poetrysociety.org.uk
www.poetrysociety.org.uk

Editor: Emily Berry
Production: Michael Sims

ISBN: 978-1-911046-02-8 ISSN: 0032 2156
Cover artwork: Sophy Hollington, sophyhollington.com

. . .

SUBMISSIONS
For details of our submission guidelines,
please visit *The Poetry Review* section of
www.poetrysociety.org.uk

ADVERTISING
To advertise, visit www.poetrysociety.org.uk
or contact Oliver Fox on
+44 (0)20 7420 9886,
email: marketing@poetrysociety.org.uk

BOOKSHOP DISTRIBUTION
Central Books, 50 Freshwater Road, London
RM8 1RX, UK. Tel: +44 (0)20 8525 8800
or visit www.centralbooks.com

PBS EXCLUSIVE BOOK SUPPLY SERVICE
Readers of *The Poetry Review* can order the books
featured in the magazine by mail order and post-free
from the Poetry Book Society. Tel: +44 (0)191
230 8100 or email pbs@inpressbooks.co.uk,
quoting *The Poetry Review*.

SUBSCRIPTIONS & SALES
UK individuals: £35 / Europe: £45
Rest of the World: £50
(all overseas delivery is by airmail)
Single issue: £8.95 plus postage.
Order from www.poetrysociety.org.uk/shop or
contact Paul McGrane on +44 (0)20 7420 9881.
Pay by cheque (sterling and US dollar
cheques only), credit card or Direct Debit.

The Poetry Review is also available on audio CD.

The Poetry Review is the magazine of
The Poetry Society and was first published in 1912.
A subscription to *The Poetry Review* is included as
part of membership of The Poetry Society. It is also
on sale in leading bookshops. A digital version of
the magazine is also available. Views expressed in
The Poetry Review are not necessarily those of The
Poetry Society; those of individual contributors
are not necessarily those of the Editor.
Charity Commission No. 303334.

Cover quote: by Kei Miller, see pp. 33–35

THEPOETRYSOCIETY

Supported using public funding by
ARTS COUNCIL
ENGLAND

CONTENTS

Poems

Poems from Poetry (i)

Prose

Poems

Poems from Poetry (ii)

Prose

Reviews

EDITORIAL

On my walk home from a friend's house some nights ago it began to rain a very fine but thorough rain and I got soaked in a way that felt like both a punishment and a blessing. I encountered a fox with a furless tail and a frog on her way somewhere, maybe on her way home like me.

Which is the thought, and which is the feeling? Lately I have been reading Judith Butler's *Precarious Life: The Powers of Mourning and Violence* (2004), her analysis of the violence of post-9/11 politics in which she asks whether there is "something to be gained" from holding on to feelings – in this case grief, from "remaining exposed to its unbearability".

When I was young, Best Beloved, I had a cat who would bring frogs in from the garden and I often had to rescue one from inside the house and take it back out. Holding a frog was a bit like holding a feeling. Special, and a touch icky, like most intimacies (like this one).

Butler suggests that instead of seeking resolution through violence, for example through military conflict, by "tarrying with grief" we might be returned to "a sense of human vulnerability, our collective responsibility for the physical lives of one another".

Was it my feeling or was it the frog's? Their skin is so thin and their heartbeat so close it's hard to tell. In this ever more precarious life I'm drawn to poems that make me feel as if I'm holding a feeling and I don't know whose it is. Poems that make me feel vulnerable and responsible.

A good poem knows how to hold on, how to get up close to something and not let go, like the photographer in Patrick Cotter's 'O'Sullivan', a few pages ahead, who "developed the confidence to focus / on the eye alone, from all angles, in all shades / of light, even in darkness", or the speaker in Gillian Allnutt's 'abutment', whose meditative inventory of feelings seems to reach beyond our sense of an individual towards something more expansive.

And poems can transcend the separateness of bodies – they can bring the inside outside and vice versa. When the forces of division rule, I want to find ways of adding up again. Audre Lorde wrote, "Kept around as unavoidable adjuncts or pleasant pastimes, feelings were expected to kneel to thought as women were expected to kneel to men." Who can say what precise configuration of thought and feeling is found in any one poem; perhaps their very relation confers its "subtle electricity" – Wallace Stevens's "thought / Beating in the heart" – like that found in Layli Long Soldier's powerful 'Whereas Statements', which call to account the legislative language of oppression: "Whereas I have spent my life in unholding. *What do you mean by unholding?* Whereas asks and since Whereas rarely asks, I am moved to respond". The Chilean poet Cecilia Vicuña reminded us once, "Words have a love for each other, a desire that culminates in poetry."

Kei Miller asks in his manifesto whether poetry has forgotten how to serve its community. A.K. Blakemore asks in hers, "Tell me what you need to look at to survive." In *Precarious Life* Judith Butler wonders, "To what are we tied? And by what are we seized?" I will continue thinking about vulnerability and responsibility, and feeling them.

Emily Berry

This issue contains a selection of poems from US magazine Poetry, *edited by Don Share. Poems from* The Poetry Review *will appear in* Poetry *as part of an ongoing transatlantic exchange between the two publications.*

GILLIAN ALLNUTT

abutment

but for the askance in her

but for the biding in abeyance of her

but for the clairvoyance that came to her like a grandmother

but for the expanse of love in her the lark in the clear air

but for the auld acquaintedness with violence in her

magdalen

the darkest hour

the stars arisen asinine

tomb and I left opened to the altogether

am I to live among men abandoned I may learn to love again

adrift in Jerusalem

am I upon strewn palm

Portrait of Hester by her husband

How well she has worn the wooden evangelist of the mind
I wrought in her.

He is fraught as Angel Clare
With honesty, with his *latchet*
Worthy of her.

When I am gone she will put him on the fire
As if he'd condemned her.

KATE POTTS

Catalogue of Strange Fish

From the un-fathomed, farthest away from the light, from the sea's
iron guardedness they come –

pin-eyed, with flesh like tree-bark. Their jaws are gorgeously spiked,
ragged with toothpick teeth, goon teeth, prison bar teeth.

O Anglerfish, Vampire fish, Oarfish, Goonch. A strange fish holds himself
upright and fast to the park railings. He is white-knuckled.

His eyes focus upwards as if counting or reciting, tugging at the brain's
stubborn pinions. When you ask if there's somewhere

he needs to get to, he only sets his jaw harder. You both know that if he
acknowledges you, he'll fall. Every one of your dreams

is about the president, however tangentially. Each morning, pre-waking,
mucid insects seem to attach themselves

to your collarbone and gnaw in at the marrow. What if we could all say
whatever came first to mind, whenever we wanted to? No

perusal. *Scullion! Arse-wipe! Warp-faced pignut!* Invincible as a body
that's snug in the womb. What if we could all get

whatever we wanted, whenever – as in the fairy tale? On the beach
at Marazion the surf is spangled with mackerel scales.

The sands heave with stranded bodies, underwater silver bullets, drying
and curling up in the winter light, so close to home.

NICOLA HEALEY

Uncovered Bones

We live in a world paralysed with principles. We just let other people die.
   – Marguerite Duras, Practicalities

Sometimes, she watched the past in dismay;
not because it was hers – not just,
but the fact of it. That a girl could corrode so –
for years. That such waste is let to live.

Time was only an acid bath. Brutally exposed,
we didn't know night from day.
Frozen nights that no blanket could thaw
without the body's first cover.

Marrow transmutes to ice. I am her sacrum,
former chalice to the soul, usually covered.
She hit me on the bath edge once – bone on steel.
I shook her with a white-hot whimper.

The feet bones cried in protest too
with fiery tear and blood. Not enough
to buffer pounding blows from stone.
A skeleton isn't made to walk alone.

She couldn't hold us up in the end;
she forgot she was twenty-nine, not ninety,
not yet. We live a covered life now,
with others like us – under the great silencer

that is the earth's flesh. You will hear tales
told with the confidence of the living
that we were narcissists. It is a self-serving ploy,
to speak loudly for the speechless dead.

Sacred Hunger

In full light we are not even a shadow.
  – Antonio Porchia, *Voices*

Buried in the dark, lights glowed so much brighter.
You climb up and out only to find treasures vanished.
All things had a presence – an offering to give:

a fairy light, a friend, could mainline hope
in a second – cracked the dark with lightning glimmers
of more, as Kintsugi solders fragments with gold.

Any flash was seized like water in a drought.
I bathed in fairy lights' little corollas like a child,
as if indoor stars could solve everything.

Light put out their hearts. I miss the austerity
of weakness, so stripped weak it transfigures
to force, as a crucible melts metal from ore.

Where are those who told me, this was the way?
Life – is a long vivisection. You are both
maverick scientist and lone animal

trapped in a fluorescent glare. The choice
was given as life or death, but no one says
the third: you can be buried in the light.

PATRICK COTTER

O'Sullivan

The man with the old Leica had just one subject:
left eyes – not right eyes, not whole faces;
left eyes blinking, left eyes winking

left eyes glaring, left eyes staring
left eyes squinting and peering, laughing
and crying. He photographed people eyes

dog eyes, cat eyes, cow eyes, sheep eyes
crow eyes. He bought a microscope
with a special lens-adapter and photographed

spider eyes – always the most lefty of the eight.
At first, he photographed whole faces
and cropped everything out except the left eye

but then he developed the confidence to focus
on the eye alone, from all angles, in all shades
of light, even in darkness, reflecting the moon.

When it came to the eyes of the dead
he had no access to battlefields or morgues
so he would steal into funeral homes, approach

a solitary corpse laid out in open casket, pin back
the eyelid and snap. Then he went to market
and captured the eyes of severed pork heads;

he swept along the fish stall snapping salmon
shark, tuna, mackerel, monk and plaice.
He processed and printed the negatives

himself on special luminous card, hung them
on his ceiling, so he would drift asleep every night
staring at constellations of eyes, left ones.

RAYMOND ANTROBUS

Sound Machine

My mirth can laugh and talk, but cannot sing;
My grief finds harmonies in everything
   – James Thompson

And what comes out if it isn't the wires
dad welds to his homemade sound system
which I accidently knock loose
while he is recording Talk-Over dubs, killing
the bass, flattening the mood and his muses
making dad blow his fuses and beat me.
It wasn't my fault, the things he made
could be undone so easily –
and we would keep losing connection.
But I praise my dad's mechanical hands –
even though he couldn't fix my deafness
I still channel him. My sound system plays
on Father's Day in Manor Park Cemetery
where I find his grave, and for the first time
see his middle name *Osbert*, derived from Old English
meaning *God*, and *Bright*. Which may have
been a way to bleach him, darkest
of his five brothers, the only one sent away
from the country to live up-town
with his light skin aunt. She protected him
from police who did not believe he belonged
unless they heard his English,
which was smooth as some uptown roads.
His aunt loved him and taught him
to recite Wordsworth and Coleridge – rhythms
that wouldn't save him. He would become
Rasta and never tell a soul about the name
that undid his blackness. It is his grave
that tells me the name his black
body, even in death, could not move or mute.

MARY JEAN CHAN

Tea Ceremony

There are days when I pretend
to understand my mother's grief –

as I coax her into sitting at the table
for a tea ceremony – so she might

linger on the rush of green into glass,
how the scent of leaf dissolves both

past and future in one gulp. We drink
in a serene silence, my mother smiles

a smile that breaks my breath into
laughter. She is radiant now, lost

in the repetitive chant of the kettle –
her gaze fixed on the dance of fingers

between utensils. I love my mother's
joy, her reprieve from the sorrow of

Red-Guarded nights. Time is a wound
she adorns with designer clothing and

too many sleeping pills. I tell her: *go
to bed*. She says: *I can't. Can you stay?*

As a child, I would dread her desperate
need, hand resting on her forehead, unable

to let go. Even now, with Freud and Jung
as bedside reading, I can only invite her

to the table: *look, mother, your hands are
beautiful. Look, mother, our tea is ready.*

what my mother (a poet) might say

that she had scurvy as a child
that I don't understand hunger until I can describe what a drop of oil tastes like

that Mao wrote beautiful Chinese calligraphy

that she finds democracy to be the opiate of the masses
that I am a descendant of the Yellow Emperor

that Mao wrote beautiful Chinese calligraphy

that she dreams about seeing her father's heart in the doctor's fist
that I must only write about flowers

that Mao wrote beautiful Chinese calligraphy

that she showed her mother-in-law a blood-speckled sheet the morning after
that I shall love a man despite his strength

that Mao wrote beautiful Chinese calligraphy

that she wants to devour me back into herself
that I would be *ci sin* to love another woman

that Mao wrote beautiful Chinese calligraphy

that her neurons are a crumbling Great Wall
that I am a new earth arising from hierarchies of bone

that Mao wrote beautiful Chinese calligraphy

LUCY TUNSTALL

Kaftan

My mother has taken me to Paddington Station.
We are inside a whale.

My father sleeps all day.
When he wakes the cloisters come for him.

My sister can sit on her hair. At night, a man sits on her bed.
Her bed is covered in oak leaves.

The sleeves of my mother's kaftan trail in the dirt.
We keep forgetting it's not her.

The telephone bursts from the wall. The wires are a joke.
We *get* it.

The Patient

I have no idea what happens when I turn my back.
I sleep through everything.
It is quite stupid how I never open my eyes.

The carpet is luscious. The blossom at the window is spectacular.
I try to keep them apart.
There are more grown-ups than I know what to do with.
I have a different *Darling* for each one. I inflect it.

I miss everything – the haunted wardrobe, the bald landlady,
the slurring woman crashing up and down the stairs,
Look after her, Look after her, Pierrot with his little spoon.

Torch Song

Anoint your dead
poems.

Put them in a little boat called
She Who Must Be Obeyed –
our little joke.

Invite the Molotovs for cocktails on deck.
Tell them to wear *all* their gold.

ANGEL NAFIS

Ghazal for Becoming Your Own Country

After Rachel Eliza Griffiths's Self Stones Country *photographs*

Know what the almost-gone dandelion knows. Piece by piece
The body prayers home. Its whole head a veil, a wind-blown bride.

When all the mothers gone, frame the portraits. Wood spoon over
Boiling pot, test the milk on your own wrist. You soil, sand, and mud
     grown bride.

If you miss your stop. Or lose love. If even the medicine hurts too.
Even when your side-eye, your face stank, still, your heart moans *bride*.

Fuck the fog back off the mirror. Trust the road in your name. Ride
Your moon hide through the pitch black. Gotsta be your own bride.

Burn the honey. Write the letters. What address could hold you?
Nectar arms, nectar hands. Old tire sound against the gravel. Baritone bride.

Goodest grief is an orchard you know. But you have not been killed
Once. Angel, put that on everything. Self. Country. Stone. Bride.

PETER GIZZI

A Winding Sheet for Summer

1

I wanted out of the past so I ate the air,
    it took me further into air.
It cut me, an iridescent chord
    of geometric light.
I breathed deep, it lit me up, it was good.
All these years, lightning, rain, the sky,
    its little daisies.
Memento mori and lux.

2

And you can't blame me.
This daisy-feeling.
I was a poet with a death-style of my own
    waking.
I occupy the rest of it.
A blue-green leaving feeling.
To no longer belong to a body sometimes
    open to air.
In rain, in early morning rain.

3

Today was the day of the amphitheater in mind.
The day of a dreaming speech where the light is dope
    and that's all you can say.
When a feeling degrades and evolves into thought like
    2 a.m. dilated, revealed a star.
It will say this long agony is great being awake.
It is being lovely now.

4

All the stars are here that belonged to whatever
    was speaking.
I built my life out of what was left of me.
Sky and its procedures.
A romanticism of clouds, trees, pale crenellations,
    and poetry.
A musical joybang.
Touching everything.

5

When the words come back their fictions remain.
Thunderheads and rain, lexical waters raking gutters,
    carving a world.
The stylus will live in the flash.
A daring light from pewter to whatever.
Now discrete observations produce undramatic sound,
    like I am a bubble,
make me the sea. O, make me the sea.

6

For a long time the names of things and things unnamed.
For a long time hawks and their chicks, fox and their cubs,
    mice and their mice.
For a long time bunnies and boojum, and a name
    for every bird in me.
I am native to feathers — their netherside.

7

The sun was a goldish wave taped to a book.
A wavy diagram in a fusty book.
Foxed old wave.
A soft electro-fuzz enters the head.
A soft fuzzy opiate lightness.
What could be the message in this
    pointillist masquerade.
What use memory.

8

I came from a different world.
I will die in it.
Someone saw it, I love them for seeing it.
I love seeing it with them.
Love watching it die in me.
It wasn't behind or beside me.
Finding it wasn't it.
Being it was everything.
That was the thing I thought as I fell.

9

I am that thing in morning, whatever motors in the skull,
    something is claimed.
Sudden rain keeps it real.
Rooftops from the window look stunned.
    Cleansed.
Looking out over the day, the pale performing day.
I always consult the air before composing air.

10

And what have you been given, the blue nothing asks,
    who are you under clanging brass?
Who are you, Saturday; sing to me.
See the crows thread summerismus.
Afternoon shade mirrors an issuelessness.
A perfection of beetle slowly treading summer's blade.
The leaves broadcast color.
I was born in summer, my conqueror,
    breaking into wisteria.

11

The sun was a golden rag nailed to a ladder.
And here the marigolds grow down to the banks.
The mayflies drowse above water.
How then the dazzling surface and its dictions
    under piled clouds,
and clouds sitting there by place and sound.
One thing. This thing and sound glitters.
Indicative transitive particular battles the void.
All afternoon a green-gold silent light
    on the spotted grass, sprung.

12

I know it's summer even if I can't decipher the call.
I believe in the birds haunting me. I held on.
I'm full of bluster but also full of vision.
I'm not ready to put the book down.
To stop singing bright spots thrilling the quicksilver
    over my torrent.
I make sounds, forget to die. I call it living,
   this inhuman conch in the ear.
A pewter sensation and wind.

13

The sun remains a yellow sail tacked to the sky.
I am climbing air here. I am here
    in the open.
The kestrel swerves.
Its silent kerning.
A stunning calibration of nothing.
I'm left to see.

JENNIFER BARTLETT

from *'The Hindrances of a Householder'*

Jennifer had a tendency to stop in
the street and listen to the neighbors'

problems. She was consoling to them.
Jennifer would look for people in trouble

and offer help, even though
her body was relatively weak, and

she could not carry groceries
for the old people, really.

When the young mothers had issues
they would come to Jennifer because they

knew that Jennifer also had had issues
as a young mother and would listen to them.

Now Jennifer had middle mother issues.

·

Everything can be illuminated by water
or most things.

The two women in the black of mourning
knelt by the river in exact tandem, and

they spoke softly.
The film, like life itself, had minimal

plot and extraordinary beauty.
The film, like life itself, was

slow and maniacal. And when
we walked the village afterwards

in search of just the right martini
I thought of the same steps I had

taken years earlier in preparation
for mourning, and I was not unhappy.

ALISON C. ROLLINS

Why Is We Americans

We is gator teeth hanging from the rear-
view mirror as sickle cells suckle at Big
Momma's teats. We is dragonfly
choppers hovering above Walden Pond.
We is spinal cords shedding like the skin
of a cottonmouth. We is Psalm 23 and
the Pastor's chattering chicklets. We is
a good problem to have. We is throats
constricting and the grape juice
of Jesus. We is Roach and Mingus in
Birdland. We is *body electric,* eyes
watering with moonshine, glossy lips
sticky with lard. We is half brothers in
headlock, arm-wrestling in the dirt.
We is Vaseline rubbed into knocked
knees and cracked elbows. We is ham
hocks making love to kidney beans. We
is Orpheus, lute in hand, asking *do we
have a problem?* We is the backstory
of myth. We is sitting horse and crazy
bull. We is brown paper bags and
gurgled belches. We is hooded ghosts
and holy shadows roaming Mississippi
goddamned. We is downbeats and
syncopation's cousin. We is mouths
washed out with the blood of the lamb.
We is witch-hazel-coated backs sucking
on peppermint wrappers. We is the
spiked antennas of a triangle face
praying mantis. We is barefoot
tongue-tied hogs with slit throats and
twitching bellies. We is sun tea and

brewed bitches. We is the crying
pussies that stand down when told to
man up. We is Radio Raheem and Zoot
Suit Malcolm. We is spit-slick low cuts
and fades. We is scrappy black-masked
coons and turkey-necked bullfrogs. We
is the pits of arms at stake, the clouds
frothing at the mouth. We is swimmers
naked, private parts allegedly fondled
by Whitman beneath the water. We is
late lurkers and castrated tree limbs
on the Sunday before last. We is red-
veined pupils and piss-stained knickers,
slack-jawed and slumped in the
bathroom doorway. We is whiplash
and backhanded ways of settling grief.
We is clubbin' woolly mammoths
upside the head, jammin' fingers in
Darwin's white beard. We is comin'
round yonder, pigeon-toed and
bowlegged, laughin' our heads off.
We is lassoed cowboys swingin' in
the sweet summer breeze.

JAMESON FITZPATRICK

I Woke Up

and it was political.
I made coffee and the coffee was political.
I took a shower and the water was.
I walked down the street in short shorts and a Bob Mizer tank top
and they were political, the walking and the shorts and the beefcake
silkscreen of the man posing in a G-string. I forgot my sunglasses
and later, on the train, that was political,
when I studied every handsome man in the car.
Who I thought was handsome was political.
I went to work at the university and everything was
very obviously political, the department and the institution.
All the cigarettes I smoked between classes were political,
where I threw them when I was through.
I was blond and it was political.
So was the difference between "blond" and "blonde."
I had long hair and it was political. I shaved my head and it was.
That I didn't know how to grieve when another person was killed in America
was political, and it was political when America killed another person,
who they were and what color and gender and who I am in relation.
I couldn't think about it for too long without feeling a helplessness
like childhood. I was a child and it was political, being a boy
who was bad at it. I couldn't catch and so the ball became political.
My mother read to me almost every night
and the conditions that enabled her to do so were political.
That my father's money was new was political, that it was proving something.
Someone called me faggot and it was political.
I called myself a faggot and it was political.
How difficult my life felt relative to how difficult it was
was political. I thought I could become a writer
and it was political that I could imagine it.
I thought I was not a political poet and still
my imagination was political.
It had been, this whole time I was asleep.

MANIFESTOS

In this new series, we invite poets to write their own 'poetry manifesto'

. . .

A.K. Blakemore
"The flower is forever my captain"

I think it should behave like the jeweller's name printed in high-gloss on the very white ring box as it is turned in the hand under the light or like the shape drawn in the condensation on a bus window early in the morning but late enough for several other people to have come and gone and fogged the shape with their breathing or an extremely recent snowfall that contains minuscule claw-prints and a single pair of boot-prints that have no obvious beginning at a doorway in the manner you would expect, or like scallops – and be treated accordingly. The word scallops – which reminds me of scalps – which in turn makes me think of razor-blade being taken to the softly furred (why furred?) stomach of a female Neptune. Sometimes I come home from work after dark and strip lights in my kitchen will not turn on straight away, but instead flash abortively, and I stand in the hallway turning the switch on and off as my black cat walks across the linoleum floor, and is visible only in these flashes, a few strides further at each gasp of the light that will not work. And I think, that is how we should move from one thing to another in a poem.

The first draft I wrote of this seemed more like *a short guide for the female dilettante*. Now I intend to insist that all it is or can be is a cotton throw whose pattern has been ruined after a thread in the weft was tugged astray by a broken press-on nail. Identify where you sit in this metaphor. I have suffered from visual and auditory hallucinations since adolescence (sounding tones when lying in bed and waking up, unknown voices that deliver bewildering imperatives, the malevolent twitching of regular patterned surfaces, i.e. wallpapers and kitchen tiles seen as though through a heat shimmer). This was a gamma-mode life where some living-room walls were an emerald fern covered in swarming insects or particles of golden prelapsarian dust that found form in the fading propulsion of a gust from the open door of a different place where there were no living rooms. None of this ever felt violent, or even particularly frightening. Some were also just living-room walls. This once fully convinced me of my own divinity, or perhaps a form of Angelhood.

In practice, you start with a wash like the one of the three or four nights of distant and overlaying frost that come during the year. Look, there is frost on the pampas grass and on the corner of the roof, as well. You must shape from the silence the nightshift walk home in. A field of purity to be disturbed as little as possible. Early mornings are different on Saturday or Sunday, and this is a different kind of poem. Imagine you have sent a text message the reply to which might kill you – you will say to your friend later, *it killed me*. You are waiting for this reply. You bunch your fingers in your mouth and boil a kettle for something to do, pretending you are not waiting for this reply. That is the state, in front of the wash. Pay attention to the shape – horizontal lines are fattening. Some words are more beautiful than others and there is no shame in playing to this. There are many excellent poems about swans in part because. Snow both hides and makes apparent the below. To etch is to place shadow on a white space. Even children can do this.

> Poetry: Incursions of language into the daily.
> > In our polychrome, not color-happy dailiness,
> > the language of the poem, if it wants to remain the language of
> > the p., will by necessity be gray.[1]

Sometimes it begins with an uncharitable thought. Or rather, following an uncharitable thought upstream to the nasty spring. As much from that as from the tender observation that makes your heart buckle under its own weight. It is late evening in Farringdon and a girl ahead of me in the queue at the newsagent – a girl in an interesting woollen hat, who I assume is French – says to another girl who is with her: "the flower is forever my captain." She says this waving a bunch of wan, crinkled tulips. A different girl spills a Black Russian into the lap of a journalist who is wearing lemon-yellow tuxedo trousers. Tell me what you need to look at to survive. I find it helps to continue to think of writing as a delicious affectation that you are not hanging too much on. Another delicious affectation is to say you derive inspiration from the graceful silence of headstones, which I do. Headstones found in a rural graveyard that you took a spontaneous walk to in order to avoid your overbearing family. *Economy and resonance.* Women beat their slippers against the doorsteps late at night. Do they still?

Tenets are: All poetry is political but to write a poem is rarely a political act – accomplish those elsewhere. These poems are a form of ceasing to exist – they benefit from subtraction, not addition. Don't be too hard on yourself for being obscure: most of what we encounter in life defies exegesis, people are used to it. But there should be a cleanliness to it – a soapstone feel ("You want to write a sentence as clean as a bone – that is the goal", James Baldwin told the *Paris Review* in 1984. He was talking about prose, but I don't care.)

If you are a woman, writing about your experience of being a woman, you are part of one of the most avant-garde literary movements there has ever been. Everything that happens in this poem is entirely your fault.

---

1. *Paul Celan, trans. Pierre Joris, 'From "Microliths"', Poetry (January 2017), pp. 405–10 (409).*

Kei Miller
And This Being the Time for Manifestos

And this being a time of incredulity, which is to say – a time of wearing soft shoes and writing big signs with big letters, and marching, hands interlocked, around the capital – this being that time, a time of disbelief, is the same as saying this is a time of belief.

Almost always, belief, or the assertion of it, springs out of its seeming opposite – disbelief. The soul, under threat, finds its voice. On any other day, which is to say – yesterday, or yesteryear, or whenever it was before the terrible things began to happen and gather momentum – belief was a quiet thing. It is not that we did not believe in things, in big things – that dignity and respect and love were the great ideals – but that they were in fact so big, so abstract, and so obviously true that it was hardly worth shouting about, hardly worth writing big signs about, hardly worth wearing soft shoes and marching around the capital for. That was youthfulness, a kind of naivety, fighting battles that had already been won, insisting on truths that were already taken for granted.

But then the terrible things happened, one on top of another, and the momentum has gathered. Black bodies, immigrant bodies, female bodies – it turns out, they are as devalued and despised today as they ever have been. It turns out the arc of the moral universe does not always bend towards justice. Sometimes it lurches us back into a time we thought was past – times of incredulity, times of disbelief, which is to say – times when belief seems most urgent, which is to say – the time of manifestos.

And so this being the time of manifestos, here is mine: that poetry, at its best, does not speak on behalf of the self. It speaks on behalf of the Other. It speaks on behalf of community. It speaks the self only in so far as the self is part of something larger. Any school of thought, any teacher, any poet that repeats that lazy dictum – that poetry is a form of 'self-expression' – they do a great disservice to poetry. They rob it of its greatest potential.

When I was younger, before the cynicism had taken root – young enough and lucky enough to be impressionable – I read Earl Lovelace's novel, *The Wine of Astonishment*. The story – a Spiritual Baptist community in Trinidad is under threat. An unjust law has been introduced that criminalises their activities, their traditions and even their beliefs. The church community dwindles. Some abscond to churches with traditions that are validated. European traditions. Those who continue to worship as Spiritual Baptists do so in secret – their services much more subdued than they had been before, afraid that their shouting and ringing of the bell might alert the police.

In the novel's most moving moment, the pastor realises that when a law is so unjust, he is morally obligated to break that law. He gathers the few faithful congregants and addresses them in humility. It is not only the colonial government and the law that has failed them, he says. He has failed them as well. He has forgotten to tell them who they were. And in drawing the most incredible sermon out of him, the congregants shout, "Tell us Preacher! Tell us who is we!" I understood then, in the most profound way that a teenage writer could understand things, that this was a community calling to its writers. *Tell us, writers! Tell us who we are!*

Does all of this seem ironically self-indulgent, the audacity that a writer should speak on behalf of his people, should give them back themselves and their greatest possibilities? Perhaps. Perhaps. Still, it is what I believe, and that lesser writers unable to do such a thing will defend and take comfort in that limiting idea – that poetry is a form of self-expression.

And I get it. At some point in the history of poetry, the poet was invented. That chronology is important. Poetry existed before the poet. Poetry existed even before writing, which is not to say that those early poems – those folk songs that told histories or that were used in rituals or that gave the simplest musical delight – that they came fully formed out of the ether. There was a woman or man behind these poems, someone who had a facility with words and with composition. But once composed, those poems did not demand attribution or ownership. There was no competition, no literary rivalries, no prizes to be won. Then the poet was invented, which was perhaps inevitable given the ways of man, our relentless need to possess whatever can be possessed. Poetry became a space where the poet could show himself off – his unique voice, his own linguistic acrobatics, his own imagination and intelligence. This isn't necessarily a bad thing. If not a divide, then a spectrum has certainly emerged. Poems that sit more comfortably in community, that give themselves willingly to the masses, are hardly ever celebrated as masterpieces in literature. On the other hand, poems that speak to much smaller audiences, to the poet and the elite group of people who read 'serious poetry', are given platitudes and prizes and platforms. Maybe this is as it should be. I do not know.

I do not write against this divide. I do not write against ambition. I do not write for the sudden democratisation of poetry. I only lament the tendency for our best poets to turn their heads further and further away from community and to speak only about themselves. I assert that language belongs to people and must always be returned to them. I assert that in these times, these terrible times, with so many bodies under threat, that the best of poetry cannot be content with writing about the singular self. In times of incredulity and disbelief, the best poems must reassert their place within community. They must approach their people with a kind of humility and say, *I am sorry I have neglected you, but look. Look. This is who you are.*

Rita Ann Higgins
Sound and Sense

Apoem does not have to be nice. I want a poem to make me think or feel something about someone, some place or thing I didn't know about. If the poem makes me feel about it in a different way, I consider that a bonus. I don't have to be able to relate to the poem, but if I can, that always helps. I remember a poem that I can enter into imaginatively much longer than I remember a rattle bag of abstractions.

If a poem can make you feel the truth of it, regardless of how the poet came to that truth, it adds to the currency of that poem. Yes, poems have value and so do poets. Conversational poems have as much value to me as the well-wrought Alexandrine. For me a poem should have an inner dance. I'm not suggesting a cross between a Highland Fling and *Riverdance*, something a bit more subtle than that, a YOU rhythm. It's yours and it relates to the poem that you are working on. You hear it in the ear first and then you internalise it and you tap away and let each word fall against the next word. If it's a wrong sound your inbuilt rhythm detector will know and then you start rewriting. If the music is cut, the dance is also cut. Too much punctuation can play puck with your inner dance. In my first collection I had very little punctuation that was not suggested to me by helpful editors. Less is still more to me in terms of punctuation, but I do understand that a poem has to be sort of comprehensible to anyone who may read it.

Tone is important too; it is a window into the writer's view of their subject, whether they are laughing or crying, or both, whether they are saying one thing and meaning another. There is room for that too. There is room for the slip-sliding of the language that is there to be played with, to be sung, to be flogged, to be robbed. Take a word, any word, it's now yours, do what you like with it. Nowhere is there is such freedom.

Something has to happen to herald the start of a poem for me, like a sound, or a song on the radio, or a dream, or a smell from childhood. I would not call this thing that happens mysterious but it certainly is unpredictable. It could be a ping or it could be a shiver.

And occasionally, the call is different altogether: Galway, in the west of Ireland where I was born, was bidding to become the European Capital of

Culture in 2020. I was asked to meet some members of the 2020 committee over lunch to discuss a project. The bid, I was informed, represented an opportunity for us to come together as a community, to reflect the uniqueness of our Galway culture and richness, vitality and diversity.

I was commissioned to write a poem that the committee may look to have me read during the visit of the judges to Galway. (They didn't.) The river Corrib flows through Galway and I suspect this had some tenuous connection to the overall theme of the bid which was called 'making waves', which could be represented through language, landscape or migration.

Letting the phrase 'Capital of Culture' and the theme 'making waves' invade my thoughts did eventually trigger something in me – albeit perhaps not quite what the committee may have had in mind. The blank page was my biggest enemy here. The more I thought of the commission the more frustrated I became. I was never going to abandon my grain of truth, which to me is an important element in most poems. Eventually I did write the commissioned poem. I called it 'Our Killer City'. It ran to six pages, carrying my grain of truth over the hill and under the bridge. I didn't feel compromised.

Over-the-top satirical poems have their own truth too; let's not be deceived by the surreal. You can hide a lot behind a word or a stanza but equally you can find a lot. A banjo of vowels and consonants can throw up a hell of a mixed grill, but go easy on the brown sauce.

I like to write by hand first. I would never show this part of the process to anyone. This is the roughest part; it allows me to get all the innards into the bowl. These are what I want the poem to express. If I had to name it I would call it the inner substance, or structure. I don't always know what I want to say, I might just have an idea that I have yet to tease out or develop. Tangents are allowed, but give them back up, don't leave them hanging there with no function like a gone-off appendix.

The inner structure of a poem acts a bit like the skeleton, to which all sides of the poem have to cling. If it is well built it will always hold. Poems should challenge but you should not have to do research to get the gist of a poem. People are sometimes afraid to analyse a poem in case they get it wrong. There is no wrong, there is only ambiguity. When I look back at the handwritten version, the first draft it is often nothing like the published version.

I am convinced that all subjects are fit for poetry; everything is usable, the unsayable, the unthinkable, even the subverted cliché has standing room, everything – save the lofty. I prefer a living language, the language of the street. Glitter is for Hollywood. Let the poems have sound and sense or sound and no sense, as is sometimes the way when you embrace tangent. Words work on their own steam; language is malleable and well able for anything that you can throw at it. Throw a chair at a word and it will still be a word. Use a trowel on a poem and you will definitely kill it. It's not difficult to make up words that will easily be linked to existing ones, you can own them. Readers of poetry will get it. I like to salute the spoken-word poets, they have their ears to the sound.

YAEL HACOHEN

The Weight of a Jericho 941

It happens when your nine-millimeter round
gets lodged in the chamber. It could be the dust, maybe,
or you just didn't put in the time to clean it.
No. It happens when you're sitting on the wooden chair,
at the crowded café, waiting for the waitress to bring over a salad.
And you notice that the tattooed birds on her wrist are flying away,
but you don't know where they're going.
I say, you notice the wrist, but don't notice the man running in.
After he shoots, you want to shoot back, but you didn't
put in the time. And now you can't get your breathing straight.
You know your handgun like you know Tuesdays, like rain.
But you can't get that first bullet dislodged.
And you can't help but think of her sparrows finally flocking,
either north or south along the flyway.

What I Forgot from My Wars

Let the night come & lay your head under
a blanket of dust. An orb of mosquitoes radios
your position. Let them sing.

Even in the desert, the white capparis flowers
hold their stomachs as if they have been shot.
The larks of your mind are still cleaning, scrubbing.

Shooting is the cleaning of black oil into & out of.
You want to place your uniform on the shelf, one
sleeve at a time. Brush your hair into years.

You trace the outlines of your breath, as you
would a child's back. Say – it's safe now;
say – I've got you. Hush your marching

& witness the constellation of canvas tents fill
with tens of girls in their cots, whispering to themselves
(or each other) the lullabies their mothers spoke.

KHAIRANI BAROKKA

Flood Season, Jakarta

When the brown tongue of water
Rises up to meet us here,
The house will be gone.
While inside the minds of islanders –
Cushioned on the hills
Of this sinking spectacle
Of cardboard, blood, roads
Twisting on each other like yarn
And neon, the flash of a
Smile for the cameras,
Journeys for food,
Immune to eviction,
The rasping grey of the air –
We will be none.
Specks of paper floating
And mooring to the curb,
Collecting under a tent
And against the grate.
While inside us,
We will never have felt
More present in the world
Nor deadened, alive to the whims
Of rivers and the sea, and bare.
Meaning bolts itself to hunger,
Like the promise of fleshy
Endless layers in a rice grain,
Soft, half-fermenting, caught
Under the folds of a nail.
Into our dreams will seep slowly,
Until soaked with them,
Paddy fields withered with drought,

Or heavy and drowned; pebbles and glass
Under trucks rushing manic to the capital,
Bringing and wresting, oil drums, men,
Boxes of ginger candy, forests of logs,
Chairs made of water hyacinths.

Ramadhan

Count on always more in the wings.
On incessant Jibril, flying down at eight
To stroke your thin cheek with feathers.

Tickling skin like you've heard
Satan teases rocks with fire.
Refuse to write the rhythms
Of prayer in italics, it's not that exotic.
This is how you got raised
And woken too early:

Hordes up-and-down with black
Peci, white mukena, scarlet
Post-dzikir sunrises, each year gone
With its month of dates in the mouth
When the dark bleeds in.
                       Television
Blaring azan and inevitable local
Waterfalls on-screen; Maghrib.

Four other junctures of daily worship,
But especially then, a small spoon after,
    Cool at the ready in sweets.

God betrays everyone fast –
One month must be taken
To try to forgive Her for it;
Sing in quiet chanting together.

Take off your artifice, throng at the table,
Solitude and quiet for every other time.

GARY ALLEN

The Great California Condor

My father, high on peyote
dreamt he was the great California condor
Gymnogyps californianus – soaring gracefully
on white-ringed great wings
above the wooded cordilleras, gulches, and the new town hall
on a thousand cheap paperback Westerns

sweeping down with heavy wings on carrion
of mule, horse, human
tearing the carcass apart with his strong talons
picking off the maggots from the rotten meat
only to realise the nauseating smell of putrid flesh
is coming from his own tightly bandaged limbs

his once strong head is bald and drooped
his eyes see no farther than within
the shaman drums he thinks he hears
is only the blood pounding in his ears
the electric fire, a blazing sun
the thermals, the rise and fall of a heart rate
soon to know extinction.

ZHOU ZAN, *translated by Jennifer Wong*

Her 她

This word needs to be seen
in order to be understood.
In the Chinese language, it's not enough
to work out the meaning
by speaking and listening. Most likely,
there will be some misunderstanding.
By comparison, it's harder to misread a text.
In modern Chinese, she has revealed appropriately
her fate, as if it were a matter of the past.
Of course, if you don't believe, why don't you
stand in her place? If you appear in the poetry
you will be located on a sweeping landscape
as if neither they nor myself have ever existed,
or else, we are omnipresent. Such absence
is possible only in imagination, while
omnipresence may exist in virtual reality.

Morning sun 晨光

Gold specks sprinkled on the tarmac
and dust on the silver remnants of snow:
on Chaoyang Lu Bei, the morning sun has applied
a layer of nude moisturising cream on the shop.
The sky's mirror surface shines auspicious.
Across the road, the cluster of condo buildings stays
in the shadow, like a late-riser's dream
intercepted by the low roars of a morning train.
Slumberous. Someone awakened by love
is walking in strides –
lonely, she resumes her sense of direction.

She smiles at the vague, empty air;
warmth in her soles.
To stay confident about her existence,
she has come up with an invention:
balance, thermometer, or the right to love.

Sketch of a Cat 猫的素描

On the narrow windowsill, it has perfected
its skill to stand sure-footed, leaning
against muslin curtains on the sixth floor.
It has conquered its fear of the unknown
although not too firmly,
while wind approaches it
through the tiny eyelets of the net,
and the morning fog spreads
onto its body, the way the invisible ebb
and flow of the tide feels on the hand.
In early autumn, such chill makes
the tips of its hair stand. In imagination
a small piece of the ocean, palm-sized,
skirts past the leaves, touching
the sky's murky grey canopy.
Its ears flag up, straight, its expression pensive.
If we try, we can listen to it too:
across the distance, a child
on this dew-suspended morning
is crying loudly.

FLEUR ADCOCK

Carterton

...Of which my experience is limited to
the wind-raked station, with Kathleen waiting
to clasp us against her fluffy pink jumper,
and five minutes in a car from there to here:

a former thirty-room hotel, twice burnt out,
so that most of the lower floor is a blank shell
and you have to walk up twenty-six splintery
stairs to the family end of the dining room

where Kathleen's son-in-law, a chimney sweep
in a good way of business, has said a blessing
over our meal (no alcohol, of course –
they're all JWs – but a laden table).

Thirty rooms are a lot, even with most of them
not yet reconstructed: more than enough to store
the entire contents of Kathleen's house, shipped over
from Australia after her husband died,

and still in its containers. Not limitless space,
but even while we've been sitting here eating
ham and potatoes, cauliflower and fish,
passing salads to each other, we've squeezed in

the crab-apple tree from the wood near Kathleen's house
just round the curve in Woodside Way from our own,
more trees, the timber yard where we trespassed,
and our back garden complete with our four ducks.

We've spooled in the track across the common
Kathleen and I used to walk over to school
with our little sisters (mine's here beside me),
rolled up a road or two and stuffed them in somehow,

and compressed a double-decker bus to fit.
There's still the school itself to be folded up,
including the playground and the air-raid shelters
under the playground (we're working on those),

and the pub on the green, or at least its back door,
where if you had money you could buy a bag
of Smith's crisps – yes, the ones you've heard about
with a little twist of salt in dark blue paper.

JAMES WARNER

Der Stimmenimitator

Mediocre writers who pass their *entire lives*
reading other mediocre writers (he said to me),
read *practically nothing else*
and for no reason other than to reassure themselves
that mediocre writing is readable,
and therefore worthwhile.
And so too painters, composers,
musicians, directors and the rest,
they all undermine their art
by this habit of *forbearing one another*, he said.
Once entered into, mediocrity
becomes a commemorating morass
both inescapable and, for those with talent, fatal.
For most, he said to me pointedly, only *inescapable*.
But for a few...
Interrupted at this juncture
by the waitress, we placed our orders.
As she turned and walked away
we followed her with our eyes.
He then resumed his familiar attack.

JOE DUNTHORNE

Sweetheart underwater

Last thing I knew we were justifying the chlorine
in your parents' pool, the summer your kinder brother
came home late, a little drunk, and slept in the garden house
with the gas heaters on but unlit, and I don't remember

if you let me drift or I you, only that I still hold
the record, squinting up from the bottom of the deep end,
heart rate slowed to that of the baleen whale,
lungs burning, eyes on fire, watching the lot of you melt.

SYLVIA LEGRIS

Cold Zodiac and Butchered Pig

Onward the fairweather spleen.
Onward the season of vent and caprice.

Giovedì Grasso flies the meat,
trees still larded with winter grease –
ice, the Dead Time, the Flensing Time.

Flirt fattened Thursday of December's gorge.
The twelve pigs of the zodiac stew the zeal,
slow simmering giddy fizzling squeals.

Uncloister the close-air surgical theater.
Ungristle the knife-jester's grip.

Let the butcher carnival begin!

TYEHIMBA JESS

Sissieretta Jones
Ad libitum

I sing this body *ad libitum*, Europe scraped raw between my teeth until, presto, "Ave Maria" floats to the surface from a Tituba tributary of "Swanee." Until I'm a *legato* darkling whole note, my voice shimmering up from the Atlantic's hold; until I'm a coda of sail song whipped in salted wind; until my chorus swells like a lynched tongue; until the nocturnes boiling beneath the roof of my mouth extinguish each burning cross. I sing this life in testimony to *tempo rubato*, to time stolen body by body by body by body from one passage to another; I sing *tremolo* to the opus of loss. I sing this story *staccato* and *stretto*, a fugue of blackface and blued-up arias. I sing with one hand smoldering in the steely canon, the other *lento*, slow, languorous: lingered in the fields of "Babylon's Falling"...

ARACELIS GIRMAY

luam/asa-luam
the afterworld sea

there was a water song that we sang
when we were going to fetch river from the river,
it was filled with water sounds
& pebbles. here, in the after-wind, with the other girls,
we trade words like special things.
one girl tells me "mai" was her sister's name,
the word for "flower." she has been saving
this one for a special trade. I understand
& am quiet awhile, respecting, then give
her my word "mai," for "water,"
& another girl tells me "mai" is "mother"
in her language, & another says it meant,
to her, "what belongs to me," then
"belonging," suddenly, is a strange word,
or a way of feeling, like "to be longing for,"
& you, brother, are the only one,
the only one I think of to finish that thought,

   to be longing for
   mai brother, my brother

JOHNNY DAMM

Diagram of a Memory

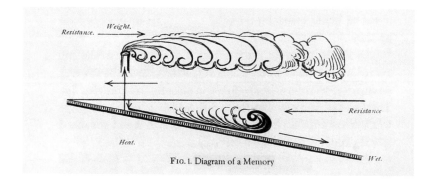

FIG. 1. Diagram of a Memory

Diagram of How I Felt When You Told Me I Look Like Him

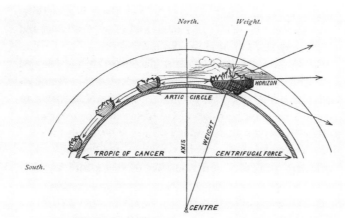

FIG. 64. Diagram of How I Felt When You Told Me I Look Like Him

VI KHI NAO

Fish Carcass

fish carcass
say hello to pork rind
+ arborio rice
while castaway caraway puree returns
home to deconstruct wilted carrot
from its butter + herb remnants

fish carcass
say goodbye to a knife fight
between under-marinated onion slice
+ wasted redbor kale
amidst a gun battle between
grilled salmon + paprika

fish carcass
say goodnight to electrolytes + magnesium
as a chemical imbalance takes
place inside the borderline cod meat

fish carcass
say good morning to anti-griddle + orange liqueur
whose pre-conditional love for salt + bitterness
reminiscent of caviar + pancetta vinaigrette
has put quail eggs
under the cloche

fish carcass
say midday to emu eggs while
the sun twirls
inside a decadent basket of
fish sauce without making
the plastic mattress, walk-in

refrigerator, + bacon sabayon
feel left out

fish carcass
say cloud nine
say egginess
say shell-shocked
say cornichon
say it angelo
say italian meringue
say calf liver
say republic of georgia
say lavash
say turnpike turnips
say succotash
say yuzu marmalade
say overcooked quail

say chef teah evans
say fish head
say into a barrel
say bacon fat
say baby corn
say flavor profile
say with victory
say the gods are with me
say no guts no glory
say did not materialize
say story on a plate

JOHN MAUCERE, *translated by John Lee Clark*

The Friend

The Friend wriggled out and stood, a smiling tree, his shimmering head turning left and right. A person came along and looked up and said, "Who are you?" The Friend said, "Come on, get a buzz. It's awesome!" The person said, "I don't need that," and walked off. "Wait!" The Friend caught up and tickled him, his fingers hooking him and reeling him in. The Friend promised he would be popular. The person said, "Really?" He wasn't convinced. The Friend poured it on, slathering him until he reeled. The Friend slathered and slathered until his head bubbled. Reeling in circles, he fell down. "Hey!" The Friend tried to wake him up. "Oh no! He's dead!" He scooped up dirt, dropped the person in, and patted it down. He acted as if nothing had happened. Then came along another person. The Friend perked up and waved.

Translated from the American Sign Language

LAYLI LONG SOLDIER

from 'WHEREAS'

WHEREAS a string-bean blue-eyed man leans back into a swig of beer
work-weary lips at the dark bottle keeping cool in short sleeves and
khakis he enters the discussion;

Whereas his wrist loose at the bottleneck to come across as candid
"Well *at least* there was an Apology that's all I can say" he offers to the
circle each of them scholarly;

Whereas under starlight the fireflies wink across East Coast grass and
me I sit there painful in my silence glued to a bench in the midst of the
American casual;

Whereas a subtle electricity in that low purple light I felt their eyes on
my face gauging a reaction and someone's discomfort leaks out in a
well-stated "Hmmm";

Whereas like a bird darting from an oncoming semi my mind races to
the Apology's assertion "While the establishment of permanent European
settlements in North America did stir conflict with nearby Indian tribes,
peaceful and mutually beneficial interactions also took place";

Whereas I cross my arms and raise a curled hand to my mouth as if
thinking as if taking it in I allow a static quiet then choose to stand up
excusing myself I leave them to unease;

Whereas I drive down the road replaying the get-together how the man
and his beer bottle stated their piece and I reel at what I could have said
or done better;

Whereas I could've but didn't broach the subject of "genocide" the
absence of this term from the Apology and its rephrasing as "conflict"
for example;

Whereas since the moment had passed I accept what's done and the knife of my conscience pierces with bone-clean self-honesty;

Whereas in a stirred conflict between settlers and an Indian that night in a circle;

Whereas I struggle to confess that I didn't want to explain anything;

Whereas truthfully I wished most to kick the legs of that man's chair out from under him;

Whereas to watch him fall backward legs flailing beer stench across his chest;

Whereas I pictured it happening in cinematic slow-motion delightful;

Whereas the curled hand I raised to my mouth was a sign of indecision;

Whereas I could've done it but I didn't;

Whereas I can admit this also took place, yes, *at least*;

WHEREAS we ride to the airport in a van they swivel their necks and shoulders around to speak to me sugar and lilt in their voices something like nurses their nursely kindness through my hair then engage me as comrades in a fight together. Well what we want to know one lady asks is why they don't have schools *there*? Her outrage empathy her furrowed brow. There are schools *there* I reply. Grade schools high schools colleges. But why aren't there any stores *there*? There are stores *there*. Grocery stores convenience stores trading posts whatever what-have-you I explain but it's here I recognize the break. It's here we roll along the pavement into hills of conversation we share a ride we share a country but live in alternate nations and here I must tell them what they don't know or, should I? *Should I* is the moment to seize and before I know it I say Well you know Native people as in tribes as in "people" living over *there* are people with their own nations each with its own government and flag they rise to their own national songs and sing in their own languages, even. And by *there* I mean *here* all around us I remind them. Drifting in side-glances to whirring trees through the van windows then back to me they dig in they unearth the golden question My God how come we were never taught this in our schools? The concern and furrow. But God the slowing wheels and we lurch forward in the van's downshift and brake. Together we reach a full stop. Trapped in a helix of traffic we're late for check-in security flights our shoulders flex forward into panicked outward gazes nerves and fingers cradle our wristwatches so to answer their question now would be untimely because to really speak to it ever is, untimely. But *there* Comrades *there there* Nurses. I will remember the swing of your gold earrings. *There* your perfume around me as a fresh blanket. *There* you checked my pulse kindly. *There* the boundary of bedside manners;

WHEREAS a woman I know says she watched a news program a reporter detailed the fire a house in which five children burned perhaps their father too she doesn't recall exactly but remembers the camera on the mother's face the mother's blubbering her hiccuping and wail she leans to me she says she never knew then in those times that year this country the northern state she grew up in she was so young you see she'd never seen it before nobody talked about them she means Indians she tells me and so on and so on but that moment in front of the TV she says was like opening a box left at her door opening to see the thing inside whereas to say she learned through that mother's face can you believe it and I let her finish wanting someone to say it but she hated saying it or so she said admitting how she never knew until then they could feel;

WHEREAS the word *whereas* means it being the case that, or considering that, or while on the contrary; is a qualifying or introductory statement, a conjunction, a connector. Whereas sets the table. The cloth. The saltshakers and plates. Whereas calls me to the table because Whereas precedes and invites. I have come now. I'm seated across from a Whereas smile. Under pressure of formalities, I fidget I shake my legs. I'm not one for these smiles, Whereas I have spent my life in unholding. *What do you mean by unholding?* Whereas asks and since Whereas rarely asks, I am moved to respond, Whereas, I have learned to exist and exist without your formality, saltshakers, plates, cloth. Without the slightest conjunctions to connect me. Without an exchange of questions, without the courtesy of answers. This has become mine, this unholding. Whereas, with or without the setup, I can see the dish being served. Whereas let us bow our heads in prayer now, just enough to eat;

The Poetry Society Annual Lecture

THE SHEDDING OF SKINS AND SCHEMES

A Voice of One's Own and the Voices of Others

Jan Wagner

Ladies and gentlemen, let me begin by articulating my heartfelt gratitude for an invitation which, for me, is rather exceptional. I do, it is true, give speeches now and again and I do write essays concerning matters of poetry and poetics, but I do all this exclusively in my own mother tongue which is, of course, German. Let me therefore add to this expression of thanks a warning: I will inevitably make mistakes in phrasing and pronunciation during the next hour or so, mistakes that may be quite painful for English ears. Now, should such mistakes occur, do not, for God's sake, refrain from laughing, but please do remember – I am German. My relationship with English literature and with the English language is, as you will hear, in more than one respect an intimate and rather fertile one – which was not at all evident when I first got in touch with the English world. I remember a visit to family friends in Cornwall, when, on a magnificent day in summer in the 1970s, we were sitting in front of a pub and I asked for a second glass of the utterly delicious, homemade chilled apple juice – whereupon my parents taught me, the six-year-old boy, the correct English sentence and sent me off to the counter to order the juice myself. To make a long story short: I returned to the table with a bowl of steaming hot tomato soup in my hands. Just as clear in my mind is the visit of a travelling theatre during the very same summer: in a paddock, under a striped circus tent, they performed a play by, the adults assured me, a world-famous Englishman, of which I grasped only that a group of people had been shipwrecked on an island that was ruled by an old and evidently evil sorcerer who at the end of the whole muddle broke his staff and drowned his books. Even today I seem to sense a slight taste of tomato soup on the palate whenever I read *The Tempest*.

Shakespeare is, as you all know, a classical German author invented by his translators Wilhelm Schlegel and Ludwig Tieck at the beginning of the nineteenth century. The immense influence of this German version of Shakespeare's works is manifested not only by the frequency with which the plays have been staged ever since Goethe spoke on the occasion of "Shäkespears-Tag", Shakespeare's Day, but even more by how naturally German language quotations from Shakespeare are shaped by German lips – and by how even imperfectly translated passages have found their way into tradition and developed a life of their own. To give you but one example, from the final act of *Hamlet*, when the hero and Laertes are engaging in their life and death struggle and the queen exclaims "He's fat and scant of breath": the word "fat", in Elizabethan times, may well have meant "sweaty" or "soaked with sweat", which could, of course, be the reason for Queen Gertrude throwing a handkerchief towards her son; in the canonical German translation, however, the little adjective is given unambiguously as "fett" ("overweight") – "er ist fett und außer Atem" – suggesting a prince with a fatal passion for Danish pastry. And indeed Bertolt Brecht, a hundred years or so later, composed a sonnet on *Hamlet* beginning with the line "In diesem Körper, träg und aufgeschwemmt" ("In this body, sluggish and bloated").

There are books so pivotal, writers whose countries' entire culture is so deeply permeated by their words and thoughts, that you simply cannot escape their influence, even less so if you are inclined to write yourself – because the language you are bound to use has effectively been created by them. In England, in the whole English-speaking world, one would have to count Shakespeare as the first and foremost of these authors, just like Dante in Italy; in Germany, leaving aside Weimar's poet princes

Goethe and Schiller, you could name Martin Luther and his German translation of the Bible, a work whose linguistic creativity even nowadays has its impact on the everyday language of people who may never have seen the inside of a church. Two poets as different from each other and who detested each other as passionately as Gottfried Benn and the aforementioned Bertolt Brecht could at least agree on two things – their fondness for well-written whodunnits and the decisive influence Luther's language had on their own. For younger poets, Brecht and Benn, too, belong to those authors you have to engage with, love them or hate them, whether you are trying to emulate or react against them.

The emerging poet cannot escape such canonical influences, but he or she will also learn to choose their own teachers. Poetry is one of the rare occupations in which, by contrast with pottery or landscape architecture, you are forced to search autonomously for models and masters, more often than not approaching less the canonical poets than the marginal or almost forgotten ones. Not seeking such paragons bears the risk of remaining forever in the realm of cliché and dilettantism. Now, in Germany there is hardly an anthology more famous than *Menschheitsdämmerung*, or *Humanity's Dawn*, published by Kurt Pinthus and assembling the poets of the so-called Expressionist decade (1910–1920), amongst them Benn and Georg Trakl. I admired them all when I began to write, also August Stramm and the ill-fated Jakob van Hoddis. My teacher, however, became Georg Heym, born in Hirschberg in Silesia but bard of the moloch Berlin. Heym died at the age of only twenty-two as early as 1912 and thus before World War One doomed so many of his companions, when, skating on the river Havel close to Berlin, he tried to save a friend who had fallen through the ice. Heym fascinated me – so much so that at the age of sixteen (seven years before actually moving to Berlin), I began to write a series of Berlin sonnets in the style of Heym. His proneness to a downright mechanical, hammering iambic line with five stresses I adopted enthusiastically – a proclivity that had irritated Heym's critics even in his own day. Today, I am far from writing exclusively in iambics; but I do recognise that many of my own poems use iambic pentameter as a focal point, they hint at it, occasionally surrender themselves to it – for instance in 'self-portrait with a swarm of bees', translated by Iain Galbraith (as are other quotations from my work here, unless otherwise stated):

a moment ago i wore at best a fuzz
around my chin and lips; but now my beard
is growing and seething i might even pass
for magdalena: all my face hirsute

with bees. how they come buzzing from every side,
and, ounce by ounce, how a person's being
slowly but steadily gains in weight and spread
to become the stone-still centre of song...

my arms outstretched i bear a resemblance
to some ancient knight whom bustling varlets help
to fit his suit of armour, piece by piece –
first the helmet, then the harness, arms, legs, nape,

until he can hardly move – who does not tread,
just stands there gleaming, with barely a hint
of wind behind the lustre, lingering breath,
and only vanishing becomes distinct.

The seemingly paradoxical last line in particular, in which visibility is only achieved by disappearance, but ultimately, too, all the other poems I have written so far, seem to suggest that a second characteristic strain in Heym's work has moulded my own manner – for Heym's poetry is far removed from anything you could call confessional poetry; he is a poet with no regard for his own person, in whose lines you will search for the little word "I" or "ich" in vain, because to Heym the "I" is imaginable only as a role, as part of an artful masquerade. The phrase "objective vividness of imagery" has been coined in relation to Heym's poetry, and, indeed, anything personal in his poetry is eclipsed by bold metaphors, apt similes, overwhelming visual images, which for me, too, deserve to be found at the heart of a poem. It would be possible, of course, to ponder whether it is not the very disguise of the impersonal, its mask, which allows us to truly and genuinely reveal ourselves.

"The first literary encounter is irremediable", the Russian poet Osip Mandelstam wrote in *The Noise of Time* (1925), and it is obvious that no one can easily get over as lasting an impression as the first happily discovered teacher. We begin to write poems, after all, at an age when we are particularly susceptible and malleable. Parents of fourteen-year-olds are well acquainted with this phenomenon. They are familiar with their son coming home at night with his hair dyed a shocking neon green because "everybody is doing that now", or, more likely, because one particular and much-admired person has done it; they are familiar with the moment when, to everyone's horror, their daughter displays one of those artfully formed tattoos barely an inch above the buttocks that have found their way into German dictionaries as "Arschgeweih" or "the arse's antlers". And even if few of our contemporaries would locate coolness in poetry of all things, it has to be pointed out, for honesty's sake, that purely superficial qualities, a certain bearing, a habitus, often play a part in the choice of one's first poetic role model. Indeed, you could argue that the immense influence that Brecht was able to exercise on his epigones was also due to the fact that he wore leather jackets and smoked cigars, that he was seen with professional boxers, that he fancied fast cars and crashed them after he had cut the brake cables to increase the thrill. And even in regard to Georg Heym, who was so much more important to me than Brecht, I have to admit that I quite liked the expressionist's rebellious posture, I liked how casually and carelessly his hat shadowed his face and that a girlfriend described him as being one part angel, one part yobbo and one part bandit. And while I was pottering with his Berlin sonnets, the devotees of Benn, as I know, were drafting night café poems by the dozen. Isn't it curious that something as marginalised and peculiar as the writing of poetry begins by adopting the poetics, diction and even the quirks of another person, by surrendering oneself to something altogether alien? Rilke once claimed that only at the end of one's life should one consider writing poems, as it is not feelings but experiences that matter. Astonishingly, at a young age, we are not only lacking in experience, we are also willing to adopt as our own the feelings of a long-dead poet.

Georg Heym, in his turn, modelled himself on French poets, and even though he has been called the "German Baudelaire" it was quite evidently Rimbaud who became his champion. Incidentally, the description that Heym's girlfriend left us continues as follows: "His face decidedly resembled the face of Arthur Rimbaud of whom I had seen several pictures." One of these pictures, we know, hung in Georg Heym's room in Berlin, and we are invited to imagine him standing in front of this portrait, gazing into it as if into a mirror, and Rimbaud gazing back at him from that mirror-portrait on which Heym, full of admiration, had scribbled the word "deios". Just like Rimbaud, at any rate, Heym introduced the hideous, the brutal, the urban and the sick into poetry; and like him Heym still held on to rhyme and metre, to traditional form. He replies to Rimbaud's famous poem 'Le dormeur du val' by adding to the French word for valley, "val", the German syllable "-de", "Walde", and thereby turning the valley into a forest in his own poem 'Der Schläfer im Walde'. And Heym's poem 'Ophelia', too, harks back to Rimbaud, namely to his poem 'Ophélie' which begins, in Wyatt Mason's translation, like this:

> On calm black waters filled with sleeping stars
> White Ophelia floats like a lily,
> Floating so slowly, bedded in long veils . . .
> Hunting horns rise from the distant forest.
>
> A thousand years without sad Ophelia,
> A white ghost on the long black river;
> A thousand years of her sweet madness
> Murmuring its ballad in the evening breeze.

Heym adopts some of the elements, the wind for instance; others, all too exquisite ones, he drops – the sleeping stars, even the hunting horns. Some things are modified or relocated without further ado – waterlilies becoming fern and weed and a whole primeval forest – and finally he adds a host of striking details, all of which affected me profoundly when I first read the poem: the rings on the fingers, the bats that, as you will hear, are allowed to flutter into a marvellous image, the nest of water-rats confidently setting the tone in the first line, all kinds of creatures therefore – not least an eel and a glow-worm. This, then, is how we encounter Heym's Ophelia in Antony Hasler's translation:

> In her hair a nest of young water-rats,
> hands laden with rings spread on the deep
> like fins, she drifts through shadows of the great
> primeval forest in its sunken sleep.
>
> Wandering through the dusk the sun's last ray
> plunges into the casket of her brain.

Why did she die? Why does she drift alone
where fern and weed and growth tangle her way?

A wind waits in the clustered reeds. It starts
the bats from hiding like a sudden hand.
Wings glistening with water-drops and dark,
they hang like smoke where the dark current bends,

like clouds at night. An eel across her breast
slips long and white. A glow-worm's light adorns
her brow. And leaves drop as a willow mourns
for her, and an agony whose voice is lost.

What made Heym's poem so appealing to me that I immediately learned it by heart was its subtle play with light and darkness. Heym turns out to be a master of a fine and extremely effective chiaroscuro we all know from paintings, for which he even renounces two beautiful details Rimbaud has bequeathed to him, namely the white lily and the veil, which we undoubtedly also have to imagine as white. Consider how Heym sets up his effect: across the first stanza he casts the shadow through which "she drifts". At the beginning of the second stanza he introduces a dusk for the sun to wander through, by which it is extinguished; in the third darkness is reinforced by using the word "dark" not only once but twice in close succession: "Wings glistening with water-drops and dark, / they hang like smoke where the dark current bends". This is not a slip of the pen; no, Heym insists on his darkness, he intensifies it deliberately, he applies the blackest possible grounding, for now, after reminding us one last time of the darkness by starting the fourth stanza with "clouds at night", it finally happens: "An eel across her breast / slips long and white" – and how it shines! A glow-worm acts as the sole source of light as if it were a painting by Georges de la Tour or Caravaggio. All that darkness, then, to render two accurately painted details unforgettable, almost burning themselves into our minds. It is hardly possible, I think, to be more elaborate. And while we are aware that Heym has chosen Rimbaud's poem as a point of departure, we also realise that he does not submit to his mentor. He is clearly a poet in his own right and, despite drawing on French tradition, or even perhaps because he did not speak French and depended on translations by Stefan George, he is a distinctly German poet, a German manifestation of his time, of *Humanity's Dawn*. Still: Heym is also Rimbaud, and being Rimbaud he is also Baudelaire, and being Baudelaire he is also Edgar Allan Poe, and via Poe and jumping back across the Atlantic there are lines leading back to English romanticism and – to name the most obvious influence – to Shakespeare, whose Ophelia has floated through so many poems and from whose *Hamlet* Heym copied a few lines by hand. So that in this utterly German poet from Berlin who died all too young we detect a confluence of historical currents in poetry: currents German, French and English. In a favourable yet fleeting moment the poetry of the world culminates in Georg Heym.

At school I was fortunate enough to have an English teacher able to transform the unsettling aftertaste of tomato soup into an irrepressible curiosity for English-language poetry. I mentioned Mandelstam a moment ago: he, too, was blessed with his schoolteacher. This man, who at the same time, curiously enough, was Vladimir Nabokov's teacher, cultivated, in Mandelstam's words (again from *The Noise of Time*), "a kind of feral relationship to literature, as if it were the only source of animal warmth". I believe I can say something in this vein about my own English teacher. Thanks to his passion it became quite natural to look over the rim of one's own tradition, for not only was he prone to beginning the school day with a Shakespearean soliloquy (if someone appeared not to be paying attention he normally shot out of the classroom only to return ten minutes later with red blotches on his face), he also introduced us to William Blake, John Donne and W.B. Yeats, whose works were far from easy to find in those days in the typical German curricula. With the years numerous poetical heroes from the English-speaking world were added: Dylan Thomas, W.H. Auden, William Carlos Williams, Wallace Stevens, Elizabeth Bishop, Ted Hughes, to name but a few. And if I am asked what I have learned from my preoccupation with these poets, I would point to the use of half or slant rhyme that Wilfred Owen and others deploy so masterfully. I would point to the natural yet playful embrace of tradition and traditional forms, be it, in my own case, a sestina, a sonnet, or even a Sapphic Ode dedicated to the quince, that stubborn and delicious fruit – from a sequence of eighteen poems on food and love:

> [...] but then who could, who would
> hope to explain them:

quinces, jellied, lined up in bellied jars on
shelves and set aside for the darkness, stored for
harsher days, a cellar of days, in which they
shone, are still shining.

Both rhyme and traditional form may be understood less as a fuddy-duddy performance of duties than as a form of playful subversion and, even more importantly, as the sort of compositional stimulus Robert Frost may have had in mind when, asked about form and rhyme, he answered to the effect that, yes, of course he was fond of using them, and he wouldn't take pleasure in playing tennis without a net either. Finally I would have to admit that, say, Heaney's or Hughes's generosity in admitting other creatures – animals – into their poetry has left a visible mark on my own work, for instance in 'an essay on midges':

[...] they form a swarm in the air,
of all that bad news telling us
nothing, those skimpy muses, wispy

pegasuses, only abuzz with the hum
of themselves [...]

Casualness in allowing even the most banal things, not only the so-called grand or eternal subject matters, to enter a poem has always, at least to me, seemed to be part of an immensely important current in British and American poetry, whether Williams praising his own nose ("Oh, strong-ridged and deeply hollowed / nose of mine!") or Charles Simic a watermelon. Louis MacNeice, whose poems I got to know when studying in Dublin, somewhere or other calls the poet

a sensitive instrument designed to record anything which interests his mind or affects his emotions. If a gasometer, for instance, affects his emotions, or if the Marxian dialectic, let us say, interests his mind, then let them come into his poetry.

All that encouraged me to take a close look at the world around us and our position in it, which is, after all, the real wonder, and what poetry is all about, even when a double haiku addresses nothing but a teabag:

I
draped only in a
sackcloth mantle. the little
hermit in his cave.

II
a single thread leads
to the upper world. we shall
give him five minutes.

Most poets, I assume, are able to name an irresistible paragon when asked. Philip Larkin for instance declared that as a young man he had been irrevocably cast under the spell of Yeats, that he even had a collection of Yeats's poems at hand when setting out to write, "to limber up". "I spent the next three years trying to write like Yeats", he wrote in a piece collected in *Required Writing* (1977), "not because I liked his personality or understood his ideas but out of infatuation with his music". Yeats's influence is palpable in Larkin's first collection *The North Ship*, but of course matters are a bit more complicated than that – if you do not, that is, as Wallace Stevens did, claim to be utterly and altogether unaffected by teachers and role models – an assertion that, like all poets' self-assessments, must be treated with a modicum of scepticism. For don't some poets edge aside and, as it were, 'forget' the first really important influence on their work? Why, for example, should you trust my own claim that Georg Heym was my most important poetic mentor? And, who knows, maybe for Heym it was not after all Rimbaud but Goethe, the same Goethe that Heym at times liked to call "the pig", because to him he seemed to represent everything old and scrap-worthy, the world of German fathers and German kaisers? There is often something dodgy about such interrelations. To explore their complications it may well be worth reading Harold Bloom's famous study of 1973, whose almost proverbial title appears to say it all: *The Anxiety of Influence*.

At the very least there will be, besides the traces you might expect and those a chosen role-model has left, traces whose origin is more difficult to ascertain; one can never be sure what reading matter continues to have an effect or has subterraneously developed a root system. The most puzzling phenomenon of all may be met while reading authors you are sure you have never read before in your entire life, authors whose books you hold in your hand for the very first time – only to find in them almost word-for-word a metaphor or a thought that you have hitherto claimed to be originally your own. Such an experience inevitably puts another complexion on the notion of originality and "Originalgenie".

So without a doubt, a great number of influences must be added to any single, dominating role model. "I love all those who bear within themselves a torn heart", exclaims Georg Heym, "I love Kleist, Grabbe, Hölderlin, Büchner. I love Rimbaud and Marlowe, I love all who are not worshipped by the broad masses. I love all who often so despair of themselves as I almost daily despair of myself." And let us remember that Larkin, even before discovering Yeats, was indebted to Auden, and that later on in the 1940s he finally discovered Hardy's poetry, an influence that Larkin himself thought to be even more decisive, for Hardy's themes were, like his own, "men, the life of men, time and the passing of time, love and the fading of love".

Are we all – this frightening thought comes to mind – never truly individual, never ourselves, whatever that means, not even when we have finally freed ourselves of the rule of our first great paragon, at whose mercy we had been for so long and by whom we let ourselves be possessed so willingly? Are poets ultimately nothing but the sum of their literary influences? I believe not – thanks to our unique backgrounds, thanks to our non-literary influences, our biographies with all their spectacular and only seemingly petty details. It goes without saying that all of these factors inform the poet's sensibility as much as their reading – be it, in William Carlos Williams's case, language from the mouths of Polish mothers (his patients), which he claimed shaped his way of writing; be it Ted Hughes's passion for hunting and fishing in the forests and rivers of Yorkshire; the landscape of the Brandenburg marches around Berlin for Peter Huchel; or, for each and every one of us, our very own, bizarre, and always magical childhood with its ineradicable sensory impressions and marvels. Robert Frost claimed that a poet develops a voice of their own "sometime between the age of fifteen and twenty-five". Still one cannot but wonder: When and how exactly does Larkin cease to be Yeats, cease to be Auden, becoming "Larkin"?

I am beginning to think that the primary influence in our writing lives, the one that forces us to become someone else altogether, is gradually modified by continuous reading, and that further discoveries and influences lead us to reconsider, empowering us to weigh up and reevaluate what we have become, until something like a distinct poetics emerges. And maybe this is the moment we realise that the quintessential subject matter is our immediate and familiar surroundings, and that we can put some trust in our everyday existence, that allegedly unpoetical material which is, in actual fact, our very own life and environment. So that a multitude of influences does not preempt originality. Quite the contrary: it seems that only epigonism and imitation guarantee the development of originality and a voice of one's own. "We know", says Derek Walcott in his essay 'What the Twilight Says' (1957),

> that the great poets have no wish to be different, no time to be original, that their originality emerges only when they have absorbed all the poetry which they have read, entire, that their first work appears to be the accumulation of other people's trash, but that they become bonfires.

On the other hand, of course, we must always remain the later born and can never exclude the possibility that those alien, sonorous voices, which we thought we had finally muffled, take possession of us yet again, even in old age. Harold Bloom illustrates this with an example that will bring tears to the eyes of Theodore Roethke's admirers: "There is late Roethke that is the Stevens of *Transport to Summer*, and late Roethke that is the Whitman of *Lilacs*, but sorrowfully there is very little late Roethke that is late Roethke."

There is no doubt that, as Eliot famously said, the immature poet borrows and the mature poet steals, and one could add that you have to borrow for a very long time before becoming mature enough to have the pleasure of stealing. Personally, I have always thought that translating foreign-language poetry is enormously profitable for this learning process, for you never read as thoroughly, you never study a poem in a more focused way than on the day you decide to smuggle it into your own tongue and try to discover all its mechanisms, tricks and characteristics. I myself started translating English poetry when I was studying in Dublin and discovered the poetry of Louis MacNeice; I haven't stopped since, translating Charles Simic, Robin Robertson, Simon Armitage, Jo Shapcott, Matthew Sweeney, Eiléan Ní Chuilleanáin, James Tate and many others, because it is the most beautiful way of learning – by engaging with the utterly different, the alien. An ancient dispute amongst translators is sparked by the question of whether the alien should remain discernibly alien in translation or not. Goethe, a translator in his own right who really doesn't deserve to be called a pig at all, not even by Heym, subsumed this in a pair of maxims: "one requires that the author of a foreign nation be brought across in such a way that we can look on him as ours; the other requires that we should go across to what is foreign and adapt ourselves to its conditions, its use of language, its peculiarities". Both approaches can attain sublime results.

Poems have an astonishing capacity to leap over borders, to pass geographical barriers, but also to transcend the confines of language and time. We open a book – and a fin-de-siècle poet, even a bard from the ancient Tang Dynasty, speaks to our heart, and, if you like, turns out to be our neighbour. "All ages are contemporaneous", as Ezra Pound said. And it is no less a figure than Pound whose preoccupation with Chinese poetry shows us how fertile and invigorating such a transfer of otherness across borders can be – not only for the translating poet, but for the entire culture of their own country and era. In 1916 Pound had published *Cathay*, a selection of translations from the ancient Chinese. In 1918 Arthur Waley too published translations of classical Tang and Song poems, adapting the age-old poetry to the English tradition. Unlike Waley, however, whom Pound, notwithstanding his high esteem for him, characterised as "stubborn as a donkey, or a scholar", Pound focused on the ideogram, going back to the original Chinese script. Reading these translations one cannot but notice how Pound's own imagist poems are influenced by his versions of Chinese classics, how similar they are in tone and image. And so Pound's rendering of Liu Ch'e's "wet leaf that clings to the threshold", and generally all other Chinese blossoms and petals, resonates in his most famous imagist poem, the distich 'In the Station of the Metro': "The apparition of these faces in the crowd: / Petals on a wet, black bough."

Not only did Pound discover his own sensibility in the foreign – he also ensured that much modern American poetry was influenced by a Chinese tradition which, as Kenneth Rexroth noted, himself a translator of Chinese poetry, superseded the predominance of French poetry. Even more astounding is the fact that Pound's dedication to classical Chinese poetry also had an immense impact on modern Chinese poetry – for his poetological principles, influenced by Chinese poetry and set down as 'A Few Don'ts by an Imagiste', were translated into Chinese as early as 1913, quickly acquiring the authority of a manifesto and influencing generations of Chinese poets to this day.

It seems that poets and their oft-times belittled but ancient art may now and again trigger tremendous, unforeseen developments – and exchanges between cultures and traditions whose importance should not be underestimated. It is quite impossible for me not to refer once more to Goethe, as it was he who, at the beginning of the nineteenth century, coined the term "Weltliteratur": "National literature is now a rather unmeaning term," he remarked in 1827, "the epoch of world literature is at hand, and everyone must strive to hasten its approach". After all the terrible wars a "feeling of neighbourly relations" should be established, not least by the poets and their mediation; the nations, said Goethe, should "grow aware of one another, understand each other, and, even where they may not be able to love, they may at least tolerate one another". A project, which, of course, now seems more important than ever. I remember clearly how on a warm evening six of us, nearly all younger participants in a poetry festival in the Macedonian city of Struga, were sitting on the banks of enormous lake Ohrid, watching the sunset and the distant shores of Albania, when somebody incidentally remarked that he was in the process of translating the works of the Israeli poet Yehuda Amichai – whereupon another poet tossed in that she, too, had started doing this, and a third said yes, he was as well, and all of a sudden poems by Amichai were being quoted in Macedonian, German, English and Ukranian – a many-voiced delight.

Goethe himself translated not only Byron's *Manfred* and admired Shakespeare, he dallied over Indian poetry, was inspired by Hafez's Persian cantos to write his own West-Eastern Divan, and even translated some Chinese poems, albeit via an English version. Thanks to his never-ceasing curiosity Goethe time and again explored uncharted territory, and one cannot help thinking of another of his observations, detecting "a temporary rejuvenation" in eminently gifted people even in old age. He, too, we are given to understand, experienced a "recurrent puberty", as he called it, and quite possibly the trigger for his pubertal creative boost lay in his dialogue with the foreign, his animated intellectual urge for exploration. For Ted Hughes, an encounter with contemporary Eastern European poetry and its strategies of processing wartime experiences may have provided an opportunity to hold at bay poetically his own private disasters and demons. In his introduction to the Serbian poet Vasko Popa, for example, Hughes perceives a "desolate view of the universe", adding: "The wide perspective of elemental and biological law is spelled out with folklore hieroglyphics and magical monsters."

It seems more than likely that his studies of Popa stimulated Hughes's imagination and were especially significant for his collection *Crow*; indeed, his description of Popa's work seems almost to be a characterisation of his own monstrous, nihilistic, trickster-god creation. In one of his rare interviews – granted to *Paris Review* – Hughes said: "Several of my favorite pieces in my book *Crow* I wrote travelling up and down Germany with a woman and small child – I just went on writing wherever we were." It is hard not to reflect that his preoccupation with Popa may have brought about such a Goethean "temporary rejuvenation", spurring him to write during his journey through Germany.

The encounter with the foreign, the otherness, released an energy in Goethe, Pound and Hughes, animating them to reconsider and reform what had become their very own, at the same time vitalising their own tradition and language. The young poet, more often than not beginning to write during their first, rather ordinary and rather strenuous puberty, may submit to their chosen master, disappearing almost completely in the process. The seasoned poet, reading and learning with self-assurance, in a recurrent puberty of the Goethean kind, may revitalise his or her work over and over again without surrendering in the slightest. Fortunate, I think, is the poet endowed for a whole lifetime with such curiosity, able to transform wonderment (which Osip Mandelstam aptly called the poet's cardinal virtue) in an ever-new and ever-surprising manner.

One can only attempt in one's own modest context to emulate these great figures who seem to be driven less by the anxiety of influence than by its delight. Some years ago I was invited to take part in an event bringing together writers, directors and musicians from Chicago and Berlin. I was asked to translate poems by my coeval Kevin Young, who looks back on forebears like Langston Hughes and the Harlem Renaissance blues poetry, at the same time going about his work with an exhilarating and very contemporary playfulness. More exhausting than the translation, it turned out, was the performance we did together some weeks later in Berlin. We had agreed to read the originals and the German versions in turn, so that Kevin began with his impressively vibrating bass voice – more like chanting, I thought, than reciting. He was accompanied by two guitarists who, to my horror, did not stop playing when Kevin finished his part and all eyes turned to me; they continued to finger through chords and blue notes – thus presenting me with the challenge not only of reading but of singing the blues in German, an impossible task. This somewhat traumatic experience resulted, however, in a brief yet fruitful involvement with blues poetry, more precisely, with a form called the "blues sonnet", which meant creating a German blues after all – whose singers, you have to imagine, are those mythical horse-human hybrids, the centaurs. The poem was titled 'centaurs' blues' and one of its lines, translated by David Keplinger, runs as follows: "where does the rider start? where does the steed end? / who can know if he is steed or rider in the end?"

He could now see, Goethe said many years after his epochal West-Eastern Divan, "that these songs [...] have no further connection with me. Both the oriental and impassioned elements have ceased to live in me. I have left them behind, like a cast-off snake-skin on my path." To gaze, at least once, as Goethe did, fully aware of oneself and of one's achievements, upon one of the many cast-off skins as alien and yet one's very own, to remain oneself so thoroughly in this process of permanent transformation – really, that would be an art to be mastered, but perhaps it is a little too much to hope for.

Jan Wagner, Self-portrait with a Swarm of Bees, *trans. Iain Galbraith (Todmorden: Arc, 2015)*

Arthur Rimbaud, Rimbaud Complete, *trans. Wyatt Mason (New York: Modern Library, 2003)*

Georg Heym, Poems by Georg Heym, *trans. Antony Hasler (London: Libris, 2004).* ©*Antony Hasler, permission of Angel Books, London*

This is an edited version of The Poetry Society Annual Lecture given by Jan Wagner and presented by The Poetry Society in association with New College, University of Oxford, University of Liverpool (as the Kenneth Allott lecture), and King's College London (as part of the 'Poetry And...' series), on 20 February, 21 February and 22 February 2017 respectively.

PROTEST AND STUPOR

Of Poetry and Protest: From Emmett Till to Trayvon Martin
eds Phil Cushway and Michael Warr, W.W. Norton, $21.95,
ISBN 9780393352733
New Boots and Pantisocracies, *eds W.N. Herbert and Andy Jackson,*
Smokestack, £8.99, ISBN 9780993454752
Aiblins: New Scottish Political Poetry, *eds Katie Ailes and Sarah*
Paterson, Luath, £8.99, ISBN 9781910745847

Joe Kennedy considers the politics of poetry in three anthologies

. . .

That the personal is always political, a notion with clear poetic implications, is something far fewer would dispute now than when second-wave feminists wielded the maxim in the 1970s. Since then, we have come, increasingly, to realise that politics shapes, and is shaped by, the entirety of our domestic and intimate lives. Nevertheless, thoughts of an all-embracing politicality can tend, ultimately, towards banality: if *everything* is political, our ability to act and resist might lose its contours, a helpless lassitude replacing activist urgency. Beyond that, there's a risk of bad faith – do you *need* to protest deportations if you're buying organic? – brought about by the flattening out of the status of causes.

It's also commonplace to note a prevailing mood of political despair over the last couple of years. Local phenomena, such as the Euroscepticism of rural England, a curdling white resentment in the United States, and sectarian wars in the Middle East have spread across the palette of gloom to blend in one singularly unpleasant shade. Understandably, poetry turns again to an interrogation of the most contentious line in Yeats, trying to establish what it can make "happen". Some might argue that poetry's sheer insistence that thought must "happen" is intrinsically useful in a scenario formed at least in part by superheated thoughtlessness; others will claim more direct interventions are required. These collections choose the second alternative, albeit in pointedly different ways.

Phil Cushway and Michael Warr's deliberately unwieldy A4 collection *Of Poetry and Protest: From Emmett Till to Trayvon Martin* is, in Warr's words, "unapologetically political". Its glossy pages unite prominent African-American poets in a format where each writer's work is prefaced by an interview and photograph. This situates each poem in a frame that prioritises the specificity of black lives, a specificity denied by the racialised violence the anthology's subtitle indicts. Consequently, the idea of poetry as protest is finessed and expanded as each writer proclaims a particular pantheon of influences and interests to be brought to bear in the resistance to American racism. Moreover, the tightly focused nature of the political question the collection responds to opens up, paradoxically, the field of poetic possibility: the challenge here is to write *strangely*, to jolt the reader from any complacent faith regarding the separateness of life and politics.

Elizabeth Alexander opens the collection with 'Narrative: Ali, a poem in twelve rounds', a spritely exercise in formal and tonal shifting. In the ninth "round" Ali considers how sport frequently puts black bodies on the line, wondering "Will I go / like Kid Paret / a fractured skull, a ten day / sleep, dreaming / alligators, pork / chops, saxophones"; in the preceding section longer, disciplined lines dramatise the internalising of the demands placed on those bodies:

> Don't drive if you can walk
> don't walk if you can run.
> I add a mile each day
> and run in eight-pound boots.

Alexander establishes a generalised tendency to sketch compositional rules or motifs – here, the "twelve rounds" conceit – and then to push against them, marking, perhaps, the need for political dissent to be dynamic. The late Wanda Coleman, in her symphonic 'Emmett Till', provides the outstanding example of this. Initially, the impressionistic narrative is fractured with italicised lines listing American rivers alphabetically, so the first interruption gives us "*the alabama the apalachicola the arkansas*" and the next "*the bighorn the brazos*". This invokes a penchant for grandiose geography common in American poetry from Whitman to Kerouac and beyond, feintingly drawing Till's death into a redemptive narrative of national belonging. But this sublimity lapses in a solitary, pathetic "*the des moins*", and seems to lose faith as the alliterative structure breaks down: "*the humbolt the illinois*". Eventually, the rivers are replaced by monolexical screams like "*murder*". Meanwhile, the poem's main thread interrogates the language used to justify the killing of Till and, by implication, African-American teenagers ever since: "he let go a whistle / a smooth long all-American hallelujah whistle [...] // but she be a white woman. but he be / a black boy."

Coleman's pliant assertiveness contrasts how racist language bullyingly fixes meaning. In a similar spirit, Rita Dove reminds us scornfully of the tautologies underpinning racial politics in 'The Enactment':

> "Why do you push us around?"
> and his answer: "I don't know but
> the law is the law and you
> are under arrest.

Of Poetry and Protest succeeds because it "unapologetically" insists on the ubiquity of politics, allowing an exploration of the territory of protest which experiments with the radical use of poetic irony.

By contrast, there's something equivocal about W.N. Herbert and Andy Jackson's *New Boots and Pantisocracies*. This collection, whose title references both Coleridge and Ian Dury, surveys British politics following the Scottish Referendum, the 2015 General Election and Brexit. Much of the writing is vague, *bien pensant*, or both. Several poems use the weathered sentimental trope of an adult explaining the wreckage of history to a child: Jacob Polley's 'I Try to Explain a Flower' tells its interlocutor "Something happens / in the dark to make boldness / necessary" in one example of a tone which is, weighed against *Of Poetry and Protest*'s ire, saccharine. Elsewhere, Sean O'Brien (in 'The Chase') and Ian Duhig (in 'The Blue

Queen of Ashtrayland') try, sheepishly, to ventriloquise Brexit Britain's hangdog soul. O'Brien runs with the media staple of a land beyond the M25 forgotten by 'elites' in "A Mock-Tudor Midland roadhouse" whose car park is "Dogged by doggers". The problem with these guilt-ridden expeditions into the English interior is that their diagnoses that 'we' have somehow ignored 'their' beliefs and convictions is a cliché which assents forlornly to spurious populist narratives. Likewise, Duhig's Eliotic description of "Ionian white" lumpenproletariat trainers is supposed to archly denounce educational privilege, but merely ends up reaffirming the social divisions it wants to satirise.

Preoccupations with authenticity emerge also in Roddy Lumsden's 'At the Standard' and Kirsten Irving's 'Chalkboard, London', which lambast, respectively, gastropubs serving "kale pesto" where "quinoa rules" and artisanal cafes displaying "award-winning coffee art". The implication is that the nation has been poncified into stupor, but this is little more than saloon-bar grousing. By far the best poem in the collection is Claire Askew's mordant 'Yarl's Wood Moon', one of the few attempts here to persuasively censure structural, state-sanctioned violence. Askew's "lights that never go out" are not beacons of hope but apparatuses of surveillance; the moon itself becomes interchangeable with the lunar-white faces of guards "trudging the perimeter". The distant causes of irritating menus or twee branding may be political, but not in the same way purgatorial detention is.

Katie Ailes and Sarah Paterson's *Aiblins* takes as its title a Scots word meaning "perhaps". The work collected here is meant to be political in theme, rather than devoted to a particular issue, but questions of Scottishness, and whether independence is the best articulation of that identity, loom large. Typically, Scotland is characterised by its antisyzygy, the historical dichotomies between Highland and Lowland, Scots (or Scottish English) and Gaelic: a number of the poems here are *ann an Gàidhlig* and untranslated. However, a new opposition is considered, namely the increasingly significant tension between a resurgent nationalism and an equally pronounced Europeanism and internationalism. Since the Referendum, many Scots have ministered to this contradiction through a patriotism defined by its outwardness; indeed, this is how the SNP have surmounted parochial tartanry. In a titular mini-poem, Stewart Sanderson calls Scotland "slightly / synthetic", calling attention to the enigma by which this aspirant nation-state's claim to singularity rests on its openness to all identities.

However, Scotland's secession from revanchist, UKIP-style Englishness can't found itself on protestations of innocence, as A.C. Clarke notes wisely in 'Viewpoint'. Here we see a Glasgow built from "ship-laden wealth" nourished on "comfortable lies", an ongoing denialism among some about Scottish imperial complicity. Brian Johnstone also takes this to task in 'Old School Maps', noting sardonically that the ongoing presence of colonial cartography is sanctioned as such maps are "too well made // to ever be thrown out". It's heartening to see the difficult questions addressed, as there are instances in the collection when Scottishness is glibly equated with identities truly immiserated by colonialism. *Aiblins'* best material recognises that a truly internationalist Scotland has as great a duty to attend to its historical misconduct as England.

Ultimately, the two collections with more clearly defined political projects seem to liberate expressiveness. The absence of an overriding organisational principle in *New Boots and Pantisocracies* sees its writers struggling with the dizziness of freedom, and, too often, mistaking the political with the merely annoying. Politics might be everywhere, but that doesn't mean that dissidence is well-served by a poetics of irritability.

Joe Kennedy is a Teaching Fellow on the Gothenburg Programme at the University of Sussex. He is the author of Games Without Frontiers *(Repeater, 2016).*

BORDERLANDS

Currently & Emotion: Translations, *ed. Sophie Collins,*
Test Centre, £20, ISBN 9780993569319

Sandeep Parmar explores the politics and poetics of translation
in this innovative anthology

. . .

The title *Currently & Emotion* feels necessarily personal and contingent. The anthology consists of twenty-nine excerpts from pamphlet- or book-length works of poetry made in the past five years, and expressly those that foreground the translation process within that time period. According to the book's editor Sophie Collins, *currently* indicates the "current cultural and political moment" and *emotion* "its attendant concerns of subjectivity and identity", relational terms that exist in a fluxive relationship to the already fluid metier of language. A pervasive immediacy of *the now* frames these translations in their revolutionary moment of "awakening consciousness", a phrase the book's introduction borrows from the American second-wave feminist poet Adrienne Rich. Just as the 1970s gave rise to a new 'psychic geography' for women writers, 2016 gave way to "measurable changes in attitudes towards race, gender and modes of representation". As Collins's introduction details, not only translation theory but recent critical challenges to the whiteness of British poetry, and more historical claims made by women poets against a dominant male subjectivity, inform the shape and ethos of the anthology.

At the nexus of the revisionary epistemologies on which the book relies – from feminism to postcolonialism – is a radical dismantling of literary translation as "the ultimate humanist gesture". Critiques of humanism and the humanities point out that celebrations of a universal idea of 'Man' have historically excluded women and racialised 'others' from this supposedly shared human experience. *Currently & Emotion's* substantial favouring of women and ethnic poets and translators (as well as an attention to non-European languages) serves as a clear rejoinder to a Eurocentric male canon of literary translation. Beyond this is a sensitivity towards the power dynamics of language – English in the context of the British empire but also as prop to neocolonial perceptions of Western cultural dominance. Translation, as Vietnamese-American writer Linh Dinh contends, "shapes, and takes shape within, the asymmetrical relations of power that operate under colonialism". And yet Collins is careful always to point beyond the concerns of language (for both the translator and lay reader) to the issues that underpin her critical interrogation of translation itself. She quotes theorists Susan Bassnett and André Lefevere, who argue that "the study of the manipulation processes of literature as exemplified by translation can help us towards a greater awareness of the world in which we live". In other words, literary translation cannot be neutral in its ideology, power or privilege. It remains a political gesture, unconsciously or willingly expressed by the translator's selection of texts, working languages, literary forms, style or intended audience. And in the context of US and UK literary markets, where translation makes up just three per cent of all books published, these gestures become even more meaningful.

Given the book's focus on the visibility of translation, translators who are also poets and writers make up a substantial portion of the twenty-nine, including Anne Carson, Holly Pester, Vahni Capildeo, Tara Bergin, Rosmarie Waldrop, Lisa Robertson and Erín Moure. Varying by approach, the selections in *Currently & Emotion* can be divided into at least one or two of three types of translation, defined by the linguist Roman Jakobson as interlingual (between different languages), intralingual (English to English, or a 'rewording'), and intersemiotic (translations between media such as the visual, aural and textual). Some source texts are provided at the book's centre rather than as parallel texts, thereby avoiding any privileging of the 'original' text and its author. Collins briefly prefaces each contribution with a note on process: in the case of Christian Hawkey's

Ventrakl we are told that the translation engages not just with the Austrian Expressionist Georg Trakl's poetry, but points biographically to the poet's tragic life, even his family photos. Additionally, Hawkey makes use of homophonic translation (an intentional mishearing that transliterates sound, not sense) and the physical object of an open Trakl book, which Hawkey perforates and then reforms with the help of a 12-gauge shotgun. Included here are composite poems made from colours in Trakl's oeuvre that generate surreal visual and sonic collisions.

> Red laughter in the dark shade of chestnuts.
> Snow gently drifts from a red cloud.
>
> Crossing in red storms at evening
> The mysterious red stillness of your mouth.
>
> Red wolf, strangled by an angel.
> ('Redtrakl')

Translator and poet Brian Henry has described Hawkey's process as "transwriting", not translation, but the clear positioning of the poet Trakl amid his ventriloquism makes for a readerly analysis of authorship. Henry's own translations of the Slovenian poet Tomaž Šalamun are excerpted from here alongside other, different Šalamun poems translated by Sonja Kravanja. Although both translators are differently fluent in the linguistic and cultural contexts shaping Šalamun's writing, across the translated work a similar poetic voice prevails. It is tempting, but possibly misleading, to draw conclusions about the singularity of authorial voice. After all, Šalamun collaborated actively and enthusiastically with his translators – indelibly shaping the final product. Still, an old – perhaps untranslatable – Punjabi saying comes to mind: the burnt rope doesn't lose its twist.

Much of the collaborative or intersemiotic work in *Currently & Emotion* is supported by a feminist epistemology of 'emotion', which advocates "sharing, trust, responsibility, bodies, process and the absence of hierarchy over dominant, culturally masculine traits that include products, rules, universality and impartiality". For example, Khairani Barokka's '12 Acres' project interprets songs by rural Indian women in a Rajasthani village into images – what she calls a "lateral" translation. At first one might bristle at an outsider's intervention in oral traditions, or question the translator's ethics of trust, responsibility and sharing at stake in the privacy of these female environments. But Khairani's project emerged not from a wish to transmit these songs externally, but to provide access to a hearing- and speech-impaired member of the village, Santia Patidar, who was previously unable to partake in this "distinctively female practice". Khairani's images are dream-like, visceral, architectural. They form visual poetic collages that are as enigmatic and communal as the songs themselves, for which we are given the source texts. What I find striking about these texts, as a female Indian reader with rural ancestry, is how untranslatable they seem, with their culturally specific critique of male–female relations, marriage, foods like bitter gourd, farming measures, and the (perhaps universally feared) symbol of the mother-in-law. Yet it may also be that knowledge of a source culture or text prevents, as much as it sometimes facilitates, an appreciation of a translation. A similar act of feminist translation is exemplified by Eliza Griswold's versions of Pashto landays. Also shared privately between Afghani women, these poems in couplets hinge "on sophisticated double entendres and allusions" composed "in response to restrictive social conditions".

> My lover is fair as an American soldier can be.
> To him I looked dark as a Talib, so he martyred me.
>
> •
>
> Because my love's American,
> Blisters blossom on my heart.

"American" replaces the words "British" and "liar" in previous versions of these landays, demonstrating a grim but canny adaptation to changing national identities of white invading soldiers. In spite of her reservations about the ethical issues at stake, Collins boldly includes these pieces here but, rightly, raises a red flag in her introduction. It is true that Griswold is not only a 'white woman' presenting these poems to an Anglophone audience. She is, of course, also culturally linked and privileged by (even if not personally involved in) the systematic subjugation of Afghani culture and society through military occupation and war.

Chantal Wright's translations of the Japanese-German writer Yoko Tawada conceptually and textually make the translator hypervisible while also highlighting the strangeness of Tawada's originals. In two columns

Wright comments on her process as she translates Tawada's work. This innovative method of response gives the illusion of a dialogue with a developing text and eschews the seamlessly constructed reality of traditional translational modes.

P hakte sich bei mir ein, it was raining, and we had only one umbrella. In America one rarely touches the bodies of people of the same sex. I missed the touching, I missed Berlin.

[P put her arm through mine]

In North America people excuse themselves in supermarkets if they get too close to you as they walk down an aisle. I realised after several months that impatiently reaching past somebody to get something off the shelf could be construed as rude. [...]

In laying bare the power dynamics of translation, *Currently & Emotion* generously and rigorously opens a space for discourse. It begins a crucial, revolutionary conversation – especially now, in our political present moment – about language's contested spaces where ethical, political and readerly responses, among others, appear like unforeseen artistic crossroads across increasingly narrowing geographical borderlands.

Sandeep Parmar is Senior Lecturer at the University of Liverpool. Her latest collection, Eidolon, *is published by Shearsman.*

THE LONG FUTURE

Roy Fisher, Slakki: New & Neglected Poems, *Bloodaxe, £9.95*,
ISBN 9781780373225
Deryn Rees-Jones, What It's Like To Be Alive: Selected Poems,
Seren, £12.99, ISBN 9781781723388
John Riley, Selected Poetry & Prose, *ed. Ian Brinton, Shearsman*,
£9.95, ISBN 9781848614888

Carol Rumens maps the careers of three poets in these
recent selections

. . .

"These poems no more amount to a biography than I do"
Roy Fisher asserted in his Bloodaxe Collected, *The Long
and the Short of It*, defending the book's non-chronological
organisation. Poets can't, or, at least mostly, don't, evade chronological
publication of their individual volumes, but many adopt more interestingly
thematic ways of narrating a chunk of the life's work-in-progress when it
comes to selection or collection, pacifying the chronology-hungry critic,
as Fisher did, by adding dates to the indexed titles.

Readers, too, enjoy a good story about a poet's progress. If the art is
ultimately a mystery, we still buy the idea that practice improves the craft.
It's a reasonable assumption, perhaps a useful antidote to the current
obsessive glorification of the new. Sometimes, of course, it may simply be
that poets are doing different things at different stages, but why shouldn't

this, too, be discerned as a narrative of development?

Deryn Rees-Jones is a mid-career poet, whose initial splash in the newcomers' busy pool has turned into a healthy long-distance swim. Her five collections demonstrate a restless inventiveness. Playful eroticism remixed with fragments from popular culture characterised her early work; then a prose genre, the detective story, opened more complex narrative possibilities in her ambitious third collection, *Quiver*. Subsequently, *Burying the Wren* moved into the charged lyricism of erotic elegy. In her latest sequence, *And You, Helen*, the poetry seems newly freed from materiality into music and biography (that of Helen Thomas) informing the longer stride and observational reach. Like John Riley, Rees-Jones releases new energies in her line through innovative punctuation. Series of dashes have striking auditory and visual effect. Sometimes there's an impression of simultaneity, events in separate lives being spliced together as if on film. As she narrates her own frontline terrors, Helen Thomas seems at the same time to experience her husband's death:

> There's blood at the throat. *Whose throat?*
> His body is perfect. Only his heart,
> as if caught in the split of a second.
>
> He gives her a look. *Pause.*
> The skies light up. Is this the way she might imagine him?
>
> Poems feather in his pocket.
> Birdsong. Here, is the stillness of --------
>
> Robin or redstart, called palely to his palm.

Where next, and in which genre, are intriguing questions in a poetic career clearly to-be-continued.

Roy Fisher's *New & Neglected Poems* begins with a breezy recent seventeen, then flips to the 1960s for part 2 and the '50s for part 3. The poet criticises his juvenilia for the lack of "a stable self", but the youthful anxiety seems, retrospectively, unjustified. Already, in the mid-1980s sequence *A Furnace*, Fisher was depicting the passage of time as a spiral, along which we regularly re-pass the date of our birth. This metaphor of extended access to energies and experiences never fully submerged can work the other way: the young are brushed past by the ghost of a fully mature self. There's an obvious 'Wise Beyond its Years' moment in a fine part 3 poem, 'Silence': "Giant legs of stone / Can become old men's / Crumpled trousers." Who observes the old and dying more closely than the young? Who sees self-aggrandising tyranny more mercilessly? The 1930s were Fisher's formative childhood years, and war's imperialisms and demolitions, from a working-class urban perspective, are crucial to his entire achievement.

It's true that different things are being tried, and there are occasional echoes of other voices (Yeats in 'A Vision of Four Musicians', Peter Redgrove's surrealism-flavoured science in 'The Doctor Died'.) But the scrupulous topographer is present: he manages a credible alliance with the dreamer in 'Double Morning' and becomes fully fledged in 'Divisions'. By the 1960s, the poems seem more imagistic, formally freer, but simultaneously pared down. 'The Discovery of Metre' suggests the discovery of William Carlos Williams. But Fisher remains a symphonic writer for much of his career: at every stage there's room for the rhythms of both prose and song, heroic topographies and mappings spatial as well as historical, and always, of course, a friendly, sharp-eyed joke. The new poems have an easy precision, and totally reject any temptation to Grand Senior Statement. Temperament overarches development: Fisher remains a flexible, canny, watchful, self-mocking, imaginative chronicler of (more or less) every local thing – no hill, street or human corner is alien to his eye. The book's title, *Slakki* ("Old Norse for a shallow depression among hills") may be telling us that the chronological depth of the excavation is less than it appears.

John Riley (1937–78), seven years younger than Fisher, shared the formative discovery of modernism, but took his explorations in a more mystical direction. His poetry describes the natural world – flowers, birds, leaves, seasons – with the attention of a Haiku master, and with the same sense that the natural phenomena exist within a vaster metaphysical framework. Riley wrote that the poem "does not affirm the reality of the world, it negates it". This statement places considerable responsibility on the reader to resist the given poem, with all its enticing detail, its sensuous voicings of language, its vital DNA-print of personality. Riley translated Osip Mandelstam, among others: a world-affirmative choice. Any good poet is answerable to the difficult in-stress of experience before sheer celebratory transcendence: such poetry may not ostensibly be religious but it already provides ample revelation.

A member of the Russian Orthodox congregation, Riley was deeply concerned with "the dream of Byzantium", the attainable, earthly vision of the City of God. The first three collections might be read as 'ways of approaching' the long poem, *Czargrad*, in which 'Caesar's City', as the medieval Russians called Constantinople, is a new-found Byzantium, full of air and light. Light, for Riley, is metonymic, less a physical phenomenon than the unimaginable personhood of God. Essentially, *Czargrad* is a depiction of the city as redeemed nature, outside chronology, beyond human manipulation. It continues the graceful rebuttal to Yeats's concept of Byzantium begun in 'The Poem as Light' where the significant art-in-progress is that of creation, despite the symbolism of golden birds and a "Golden throne lowered through the ceiling". What Riley says elsewhere about darkness is scathingly instructive: "a purple-black hand stretches and fills the sky: / The mythopoeic faculty at work" ('Of the Baroque').

To read Riley's poetry, however little one shares the theology, is to be drawn into participation in a pilgrimage. The music is exquisite. Elegantly cadenced melodic lines seem formed by the combined breath of Russian Orthodox choristers and Black Mountain poets. A further refinement is the unique punctuation, discovered in his fourth collection, *Ways of Approaching*, which gives the punctuation-point, a comma or full-stop, an extra space on each side, lengthening its silence, but ensuring that there's a rhythmic pulse faintly audible in that silence.

As a love-poet, Riley tends to merge profane and sacred love, the vision and the visible, and it's as if language itself refused the user's instruction to negate the observing self:

> the people inside in the rain
> look out in the atmosphere of breath and bedroom:
>
> framed in the window they see the blackness framed
> hear breathing and draughts of air and the moon the moon
> white or yellow or blood-red or the window
>
> is a mirror and two people are
> separate, see their night selves on the other side [...]
>   ('open house')

These lines would not be out of place in a poem by Roy Fisher or Deryn Rees-Jones.

Riley's art of the sacred does not finally push nature, culture and history beyond the reach of aesthetic pleasure. While his work is lodged in a small space of time – little more than a decade's worth of years between the mid-1960s and his terrible death at the hands of muggers in the late '70s – his poetry moves and lives in a long future beyond the brief time of its making.

Carol Rumens's recent collection, Animal People, *is published by Seren.*

MY DIRTY SECRET

Eileen Myles, I Must Be Living Twice: New and Selected Poems 1975–2014, *Serpent's Tail, £14.99,* ISBN 9781781257364

Prudence Chamberlain considers sex, death and physicality in a body of work by America's 'rock star of poetry'

. . .

"There is an argument / for poetry being deep but I am not that argument" writes Eileen Myles in 'A Poem'. 'I' is the poetry of surfaces; poems are the denial of depth; Eileen Myles is a protest and refusal, stepping over and through identity like a city landscape. The poet has been described as gritty, muscular, marginalised, the rock star of contemporary poetry, punk, restless, plain-talking, honest. More recently, there's been a tendency towards premature eulogising: Myles has suddenly received fame that seems long overdue, inspiring a character in the award-winning series *Transparent* (2016–), as well as a punk septuagenarian poet played by Lily Tomlin in the movie *Grandma* (2015). It's easy to mythologise Myles: the poet once ran for president as an independent candidate, had an affair with Bernadette Mayer and her husband, was central to the St Mark's poetry scene, and has had a number of publicly documented relationships. But Myles's true heroism and heft comes from their writing (Myles uses the gender-neutral pronoun), the porny-wet movement of lyric, the voice of the American loser that comes without volume control, that strident tonality that announces "I am not / alone tonight because / we are all Kennedys. / And I am your President" ('An American Poem').

Myles's work, when collected together, reads as a tireless questioning of poetry, the poet, the 'I', and Eileen. Is Eileen a figure or a form of its own poetic reality? The poems each constitute a fleshy and lived experience, performing the page and the reader with a breathless mobility. In 'The Poet', Myles writes, "I made myself into a poet because it was the first thing I really loved. It was an act of will." For a reader, *I Must Be Living Twice* is an act of learning love, being willingly led through the making of one of our most formidable poets. The wilfulness of the speaker, evident from the earliest collection and up to the most recent poems, gives the whole collection a compelling vigour and bravado. 'The Poet' continues, "A woman made me ache, I was love on the page not yet I had always felt like a brick shit house. I was the poem." Within the solidness there is still a deft movement, the lightest of touches; a technique that almost feels physical.

You can read Eileen Myles as though the work were a series of rooms. Maybe a house or a gallery, some kind of labyrinth of doors and parties. In *Inferno: A Poet's Novel*, Myles writes, "I understood community. Going to the place and standing around. Aiming for a connection to bodies, language and the future." In *I Must Be Living Twice*, we find new poems in conversation with selected work from ten previous collections. The collection is experiential, like walking into the place and not just standing around, but feeling magnetised by the body that is taking shape there. Reading Myles is the best kind of community, one speaking truth and beauty, kind of referencing Keats but dismissing his gravitas in sleights of queer slipperiness. The connections found in *I Must Be Living Twice* are urbane and forceful in their humanity.

It's also possible to read Myles as a form of sex. The collection as a whole feels like the embodiment of lines from 'Peanut Butter': "I am always hungry / & wanting to have / sex. That is a fact." This hunger and wanting take shape in the poems as we read them, and the appetite increases as the collection progresses. Meanwhile, Myles recognises in the poem 'Maxfield Parrish', "Often I turn on people / in rather strange & / inexplicable ways". It is the inexplicable that is so intoxicating in Myles's writing – the reader can follow the poems, but never quite keep up with their pace and intensity. In a recent interview with Ben Lerner, Myles describes their line as a sign "just to take this much in and keep moving", and so we do. Take in as much as you can, open yourself to a vulnerable kind of reading, while Myles – with a swaggering, butch magnificence – moves two paces ahead.

Sex also runs through the collection in a more thematic sense. 'Porn Poems' describes a tongue and heart "throbbing / in the holster / of her pussy", while 'I always put my pussy...' describes a lover's anatomy as liking coffee, having a sense of humour, as a flag that can be held up to keep us safe. The voice of the collection is often pulsing and genital, a tongue and a heart throbbing. In spite of this visceral energy, it's still impossible to pin the 'I' of Myles's poems in place. Is it a heart throb (probably), or a tongue as quick on the draw as a gun? Could it be a highly caffeinated sense of humour or actually a flag to which we can all pledge allegiance, Kennedys together?

Despite spanning decades' worth of writing, *I Must Be Living Twice* is cohered through several other recurrent themes: death, trees and dogs. Myles invokes their first dog, Rosie, a pit bull traveller of ferocious companionship; the furred configuration of trees that leaf and lose their leaves, lining the cities with their bodies; and death, which will come with the same inevitability as poetry. The hope is that death might just be deferred by the poetry, if we're lucky. And this deferral does seem almost possible. These selected poems are perfectly curated to give insight into an almost historical body of work, while maintaining the transparent elusiveness of 'I' and Eileen.

In *Inferno* Myles acknowledged: "My dirty secret has always been that it's of course about me." There is plenty of truth, divulgence and divergence in *I Must Be Living Twice*, replete with a dirt that exists without shame. The only question left for the reader is what actually constitutes this 'me': the 'I' of the dirty secret. Is the collection an 'I', or Eileen? And who are they both, after all? A tone, a shift, movement, sex? The brick shit house of the poem? The dirty secret becomes the reader's own: we can inhabit the figure of the poems, if only for a breathless moment, ever scrabbling for footholds. Eileen Myles emerges as nothing other than Eileen Myles, impossibly recognisable, distinctive, their own staked claim to language and poetry.

Prudence Chamberlain is a lecturer in Creative Writing and Poetry at Royal Holloway, University of London, specialising in flippancy and feminism.

ACTS OF LOVE AND REBELLION

Joan Margarit, Love Is a Place, *trans. Anna Crowe, Bloodaxe, £12,*
ISBN 9781780373287
Luna Miguel, Stomachs, *trans. Luis Silva, Scrambler, $15,*
ISBN 9780578173443

Trevor Barnett considers two distinctive Spanish poets
in translation

. . .

English readers would be forgiven for thinking that the only Spanish poetry being written today comes from Barcelona, and that the only current poetry from Spain worth reading is in Catalan. This is largely due to the Institut Ramon Llull, Catalonia's version of the British Council or the Cervantes Institute, which funds the translation of Catalan writers. Over recent years a number of important Catalan poets – Pere Gimferrer, Gabriel Ferrater, Maria-Mercé Marçal – have appeared in English translations; Joan Margarit alone has had three poetry collections and one book of essays translated in the last decade. Their fellow poets writing in Spanish must look on in envy. Indeed, in the same period, Luna Miguel has been one of the few contemporary poets from Spain to be published in an English translation.

Joan Margarit is one of the great poets of his generation, and is venerated not only in his home region of Catalonia, but also everywhere else in Spain.

He has found a loyal readership in the UK largely thanks to the care and craft of Anna Crowe, who has translated all three books that Bloodaxe has published: *Tugs in the Fog* (2006), *Strangely Happy* (2011), and now *Love Is a Place* (2016). This new book, with its strikingly beautiful cover photograph, contains poems from Margarit's last three collections. In it he travels across familiar territory of death, loss, love, memory, and solace.

In Margarit's voice there is something akin to Thomas Hardy, a poet whom he has translated with Sam Abrams into Spanish. Melancholy, sage and colloquial, Margarit's poems enclose a world into which the reader steps: each word leads a lightly worn path around places and experiences in which we feel a sense of belonging. This is a writer we trust. His poems illuminate and nourish; to use his metaphor in 'On the ground', each poem is "a brightly lit window in a dark street". In his work there is a quiet, emotional integrity – what Sharon Olds in the foreword calls his "unflinchingness" – combined with an exquisite free verse structure. In one poem, 'The Holocaust Museum, Jerusalem', he writes,

> I thought of Joana. Dead children
> are always inside that same darkness
> where memories are lights and the lights are tears.
> I am too old not to weep for them all.

Juxtaposing the memory of his dead daughter (an important motif in his work) with the collective memory of the Holocaust and casting it in this simplistic imagery is haunting. In Margarit's *ars poetica*, *New Letters to a Young Poet* (2011), he writes of how he uses his "emotional intelligence" to steer his poems away from romanticism. Such earnestness often leads to painful truths in *Love Is a Place*. He ends one poem, 'Classicism', describing how ageing takes its toll in lines that almost echo Larkin:

> That's why now I live in a place
> where only money counts,
> just enough to buy a solitude
> that resembles love. And which perhaps is love.

Margarit is a master of last lines. Anna Crowe's skill as a translator has allowed her to capture their rhetoric and their rhythms in natural cadences. 'The last time', one of a number of elegies in this book, for example, ends with a description of his final farewell to the jazz critic Javier de Cambra:

> We said goodbye not knowing
> that between him and me there would be nothing but
> the bad news and a poem.

The poet mulls over "bad news" throughout this book: the shadows and solitudes of illness, death, and age. Margarit, whose premature *Collected Poems* was recently published in Spain in Catalan and Spanish, is frequently looking back, as he writes in 'A sentimental tale from memory', in order to "re-learn everything". In spite of the fact that these memories include the Spanish Civil War, and the illness and death of his daughter, there is a surprisingly hopeful tone to many of his poems. These pages are filled with love, music, nature and numerous sources of light. *Love Is a Place* was one of the best collections of translated poems I read last year.

Luna Miguel is another poet based in Barcelona who has also begun to develop a following in the UK and beyond. She is a rare find – a young, up-and-coming Spanish writer translated into English – for which we should be grateful to Scrambler Books, a small independent publisher based in California. *Stomachs* is Miguel's second book of poems translated into English: her first, *Bluebird and Other Tattoos*, was released by the same publisher in 2011. In this new book Miguel continues to develop her thistly voice and to thrust her politics into verse. Although both poets write in free verse, the measured poetry of Margarit could not be further from the jaggedness and vim of Miguel's poems. Indeed, the tone of Miguel's book is set by the violent cover photo which shows a female nude tearing open her stomach.

Miguel is drawn towards provocative material. She has appeared on the cover of an anthology of poems about menstruation with blood smeared over her face, and she raised a few eyebrows in Spain earlier last year and caused a brief media brouhaha when Facebook censored her account because she had posted images of her newly published book on female masturbation. In *Stomachs* she continues to foreground the female body, as seen here in an extract from 'The Northern Goshawk':

> I understand: and I'll wash my vagina in bleach. I'll
> scrub my vagina in bleach so my kids will be born
> whole.

In 'The Light Falls Like Acid', a prose poem, she writes, "We paint our faces with cancer blood. With bits of cockroach." Her use of imagery can be powerful, but as with some of Plath's most shocking imagery, Miguel risks alienating some readers.

It is clear from this collection that Miguel is channelling into the recent re-emergence of gender politics in the Spanish media and in Spanish political discourse, but that she is also drawing from much deeper wells of influence. Although an active member of the Alt Lit community, many of her allusions and citations come from canonical writers. Her poetry is part of a tradition of tough female voices; her work shares the same DNA as Emily Dickinson, Adrienne Rich, Anne Sexton, Sylvia Plath and Anna Akhmatova. Miguel's feminism is on display everywhere in the collection. She compares herself to cockroaches, roadkill and in 'Definition of the Abdomen' she becomes a "pet":

> I am the pet and the pet takes herself out for a
> walk
> in an act of rebellion. The pet has never seen
> summer.
> The pet eats herself in an act of love.

Miguel's enjambment and imagery can combine to powerful effect, as in 'Antonio Doesn't Eat Meat':

> Like all the crushed birds on the road all
> I want to be is a dry hole, a comprehensible
> hole.
> Like the crushed birds I want to be a
> savage and a queen.

In one sequence of poems Miguel juxtaposes male figures with images of meat: vegetarianism and feminism become indistinguishable. Some of the finest poems here, though, are the elegies for the poet's mother, Ana Santos Payán. These poems display Miguel's precision with language and her control of text and space on the page, as can be seen in part IV of 'Epilogue':

Ana,
Countess Morphine.
Ana,
the worshiper of Astarte.

Ana,
watching over the stars.

Ana,
head shaved, soldier of Rimbaud.

Unlike Margarit's *Love Is a Place*, Miguel's *Stomachs* is a dual-language edition which is beneficial for readers keen to approach the original text, although for less adventurous readers such editions can create a nagging thought that a perfect form of the poem we have in front of us exists just out of our reach. The translator, Luis Silva, has done an excellent job in replicating the rhythms and sound devices from the original poems, but a few inexplicable changes and errors stick out, for example, in citations or in titles, and he appears indecisive about whether to follow Miguel's sometimes radical punctuation. Nevertheless, this collection will undoubtedly attract new readers to the work of this powerful, venturous Spanish poet.

Trevor Barnett is a teacher of English and he writes about poetry in translation. He lives in Marbella, Spain.

UNDER THE BRIDGE

Al-Saddiq al-Raddi, Monkey at the Window, *trans. Sarah Maguire and Mark Ford, Bloodaxe, £12*, ISBN 9781780372723
Adnan al-Sayegh, Pages from the Biography of an Exile,
trans. Stephen Watts and Marga Burgui-Artajo, Arc, £10.99
ISBN 9781910345184

M. Lynx Qualey considers the many hands at work behind two
collections of Arabic poetry in translation

. . .

These two new collections of translated Arabic poetry represent the
work of eight different translators: five 'bridge' workers and three
English poets. Both are bilingual, with English as the dominant language.

Bridge translations are used primarily with poetry in non-European
languages. They put the poem in the hands of a fluent speaker, who
renders it into English before it's given to a target-language poet for
editing. Facing-page editions are also a growing trend in translated Arabic
poetry, encouraging readers to see the English in the immediate context
of its 'original'. The bilingual reader jumps from one side to the other:
comparing, considering what might be done differently. Even the non-
Arabic reader, for whom the language stands as object, can at least check
formatting and punctuation. For better and worse, this structure shapes
a reader's and a translator's choices.

In the case of *Pages from the Biography of an Exile*, collaboratively translated by poet Stephen Watts and Arabist Marga Burgui-Artajo, the constraint might work to the collection's benefit. In his introduction, Watts writes about why he's attempted to bring Arabic into the English, using close translation to 'break' the English. He refers to a tight collaboration between the author and two translators, and how they test-drove the translations in live readings, gauging the reaction of the audience, listening "to the weight of our words in the air".

Moreover, *Pages from the Biography of an Exile* is so relentlessly forward-moving that the reader has little time to pause and look at the Arabic. The poems begin in the 1980s, when the narrator was a conscript in the eight-year Iran–Iraq border war. They follow him as he speaks against power, considers exile, and finally leaves Iraq for cold and distant Sweden, and later for England. The collection leaps from place to place, and sometimes circles back in time. Yet there is a powerful narrative arc, a character who comes into being.

From the start, *Pages* grabs the reader by the back of the neck and takes them into the smells and confusions of war. These poems are raw, panting, sometimes awkward, and throw the reader from the battlefield to home and back. The first poem, 'The Sky in a Helmet', is filled with gaps and ellipses:

> 'Daddy, when are you coming back?'
> I turned round...
> The sergeant yelled, 'This is your homeland now...'
> my heart shuddered, white with weakness
> I choked with tears of humiliation:
> O sky of Iraq
>   is there air to breathe?
> I looked everywhere.

Humiliation is a leitmotif, although it's leavened by the book's humour, which first appears fittingly in a short poem written in Cairo, one of the capitals of Arab comedy. 'Absence' takes the narrator off to an exile in his dreams, where he's woken by customs men at the border:

> It was then that he realized the bartender
> Was shaking him roughly:

Where are you off to in your dreams
You with your bill not yet even paid.

The collection also gives us an idea of the delicate position of the Iraqi poet in the second half of the twentieth century. In 'Me and Hulaku', a poem that addresses the thirteenth-century Mongol ruler, al-Sayegh layers the difficulties of the medieval and the contemporary Iraqi poet. The narrator-poet is confronted by Hulaku, who wants to know why the poet hasn't sung any of his glories. The poet protests that he writes free verse. Hulaku tells the executioner:

'Teach him how to write columnar poetry by bisecting his head
into its first and second hemistich
and take care not to break his caesura
and beware of prosodic and metric infidelities.'

The poem layers the threatened thirteenth-century poet with the threatened twentieth-, dictator over dictator. Poetry is, after all, still used by Iraqi rulers to bolster their claims to authority. Iraqi poet Fadhil al-Azzawi likes to recall how, as a boy, he informed his mother of his desire to be a poet. According to him, she scoffed, "And what is the real job of the Arab poets? Nothing but selling their praise poems, full of lies, to this sheikh or that governor, to this vizier or that king."

Al-Sayegh's personal poetry is part of the movement away from praising viziers and kings, as well as away from grand narratives and social causes. As the collection takes us to a permanent exile in Europe, the narrative voice changes, growing both more frenetic and lonely. "Who will protect me from cold and fatigue and prying eyes? / Lonely I gulp down boredom and the dregs left on bar tables" ('Pages from the Biography of an Exile'). Many of the poems reflect the narrator's relationship to the cities in which they were written. In Beirut, in section 12 of 'Pages from the Biography of an Exile' (the poem that gives the collection its title), the narrator rubs himself "against the buttocks of plump girls at bus stops" – a raw sexual aggression that appears only in the culturally liberal Beirut.

Finally, in London, the poet-narrator arrives at a new self. Here, we find poems that foreground an interest in religion. On their own, these short poems are the least meaningful part of the collection. But as part of the journey, they are a stark shift, an interesting resolution.

Ultimately, the 'bridge' metaphor doesn't do this translation justice. A bridge can indicate a positive link between otherwise disparate locations, but it also harks back to Cherríe Moraga and Gloria E. Anzaldúa's *This Bridge Called My Back: Writings by Radical Women of Colour* (1981). Indeed, there is hierarchy implicit in the idea of the bridge translation. Both Watts and the poet Sarah Maguire, in her introduction to al-Raddi's *Monkey at the Window*, refer to the first step in their translations as a 'literal'. It's hard to know what the concept of literalness means in this context. We might imagine what the Arabist-translator does as a first draft; as such, it is definitive in the territory it stakes out in English. The Arabist's interpretive choices are passed on to the 'poet', who might challenge or re-vision them, but these interpretive choices are the primary lens through which the poem is seen.

In *Monkey at the Window*, there is less unity to the project, both because of the nature of the poems selected, and also because there are four first-draft translators in addition to the two poet-translators listed on the cover, Maguire and Mark Ford. Five poems come from al-Raddi's Ted Hughes Award-shortlisted collection *He Tells Tales of Meroe: Poems for the Petrie Museum*, written during his residency there. The others are undated.

Many are quiet, careful poems, with none of the raw scream of al-Sayegh. They are part of the movement away from grand narratives, and some have an echo of the Syrian poet Adonis, but with imagery from Sudan. Here, instead of being swept along by a loud passion, the reader must wait for the moments of transcendent charm, as in the titular childhood poem:

> He wets himself
> With laughter
> Running through Eternity –
> Through this alleyway
> This pack of dogs
> The conspiracies of fate!

('A Monkey at the Window')

Like Iraqi poet Saadi Youssef, al-Raddi finds joy in small observations from nature, as when "A bird enters spring / like a lance" or when "Suddenly – a small fox, playful, / floods your wounded heart with joy". There are several strong poems in the collection, particularly longer ones such as 'Poem of the Nile', which manages a panorama of Khartoum through and beyond time where "all they can say to our children is: patience. / They fade into the trees, commit suicide". But there is also a hopscotch-effect that works against the collection's gaining momentum, impeding the poems' conversation with one another.

Bridge translations like these are unquestionably a boon for the English-language poet who works closely with a language they don't know. Collaborative translations, done right, are also a boon for the reader, allowing each participant in the translation to question the next, to bring the writing into sharper relief. Still, we must certainly get rid of the idea of a bridge, and of the hierarchy between a 'literal' and a 'poem'.

M. Lynx Qualey is editor-in-chief of ArabLit, *an online magazine with a focus on Arab literature and translation, shortlisted for a 2017 London Book Fair award.*

NO BETTER MEASURE

Roy McFarlane, Beginning With Your Last Breath, *Nine Arches*,
£9.99, ISBN 9781911027089
Safiya Sinclair, Cannibal, *University of Nebraska Press, $17.95*,
ISBN 9780803290631
Rebecca Watts, The Met Office Advises Caution, *Carcanet, £9.99*,
ISBN 9781784102722

Kayombo Chingonyi explores the varying projects of three
debut collections

. . .

As well as being an elegy to the poet's mother, *Beginning With Your
Last Breath* is a personal account of growing up in Wolverhampton
as a black man in the decade of Thatcher. Grief, as Max Porter and Denise
Riley have recently reminded us, can be a particularly fruitful subject for
poetry. This, and McFarlane's singular vantage point, gave me high hopes
for this collection. Unfortunately I was disappointed. Though I experienced
several moments of recognition as I read the book there were a few things
getting in the way of my enjoyment of the book as a whole.

One particular issue is its lack of lexical economy. Sometimes there is an
imprecision that undermines the mood a poem is attempting to conjure,
and at other moments a baggier phrase is used where a pithier one would
serve the poem better:

It was the way you used to put your tights on,
after a moment of loving
    or at the dawn of a new morning.
There was nothing more sensual
    or visual [...]
                ('As I did the night before')

I found my father's love letters
in strange and obscure places,
hidden in dark secret spaces
                ('I found my father's love letters')

Perhaps because the poet is aiming to be understood by as many people as possible, the diction is rarely stretched beyond the commonplace. Where the problem arises is that while the subjects explored are complex (adoption, marriage and separation, racialised violence, sexuality), their evocation belies this complexity, robbing the poems of their full expressive range. Perhaps it is too much to expect a book of poems to refresh a reader's sense of the possibilities of language at every turn, but where a poet engages with subjects so layered as those explored in this book, the descriptive, anecdotal mode can only cover so much ground.

Curiously, my sense of disappointment was magnified by the book's successes – of which there are several, including 'The beauty of a scar', 'Leaves are falling', 'The map of your leg', and the title poem 'Beginning with your last breath':

If poetry could take the pain away
it would begin with your last breath [...]
I'd be holding you close to my chest
like an accordion watching the bellows
of your lungs being pushed and pressed
to hear one last sweet melody.

These poems show off McFarlane's gift for crafting memorable images – making the personal resonant for the reader as well as the poet – but they also throw the weaker moments in the book into sharp relief. If we compare the above passage to that quoted earlier, containing the line "There was nothing more sensual / or visual", we could be reading work by two different poets. Doubtless there is an audience – maybe even a large one – who will appreciate those aspects of the book I've criticised because these moments strike an emotional chord, I just can't help lamenting the gulf between the book as it might have been and the book as it is.

Like McFarlane, Safiya Sinclair's *Cannibal* reflects on the role of racial and cultural identity in the process of socialisation. Sinclair's subject, however, is the Jamaica of her upbringing as well as her adopted home in America. Given the chimerical nature of these geographical and imaginative spaces, it's apt that Sinclair favours a ludic, continually shifting, poetic voice:

> Circumstance has made us strangers here,
> wild dance we are slowly forgetting; what home.
> The Mobay sky a lingering torch to mutiny. Rebellion.
>   ('Dreaming In Foreign')

That this poem is written 'after Caliban' makes sense in the wider context of the book with its manifold interrogations of the image of an uncouth/uncultured 'native' that figures so prominently in the justification of imperialism. Indeed, the first poem in the book, 'Home', sets out the precarious position of those travelling back 'home' to find that their new mannerisms are not aligned with those they left behind:

> My diction now as straight
> as my hair; [...]
>   ('Home')

This friction and its influence on one's outward appearance is also the focus of the poem 'Good Hair', which exposes the violence that black women enact on their hair in order to shake off the associations of 'wildness' or 'messiness' it holds in societies that see curly hair as something that needs to be 'tamed'.

The double-bind of blackness and womanhood is at the heart of many of the book's most evocative moments. The following passage is especially powerful:

> I had known what it was to be nothing.
> Bore the shamed blood-letter of my sex

like a banishment; wore the bruisemark
of my father's hands to school in silence.
('Autobiography')

The idea of 'being nothing' is here understood as a process made possible by shame, particularly in its internalised form. So, while the poem highlights physical injuries it addresses emotional ones, too. In so doing, the poem gives the reader insight into an interior world they may never have experienced. That the 'silence' is finally being broken illustrates the important work that Sinclair is doing in this book.

Of the three poets under discussion, Rebecca Watts seems most interested in the idea of a poetry collection as a set of freestanding poetic structures. Though there are threads woven throughout, there isn't the same sense of arc that the other two books have. This is effective in the sense that it allows Watts space to wander off-topic, taking in such subjects as Dr Johnson's supposed addiction to milk, figures from the Hunterian Museum, and ornate lettering in ancient manuscripts. It is not always clear what each poem might be contributing to what the book as a whole is trying to 'say' but that's not to suggest that nothing is being said.

One of the book's discernible concerns is with the shifts in human relationships:

[...] everything leads back to something. Like us
one weekend, scanning thirty-six miles of pavement, canal-side,
verge, forgotten garden in search of your dropped wallet
('The Ways')

The parents don't know how to party.
They're yawning and hating each other.
('Party')

In 'The Ways', the communion with nature begins as a communion between two people wandering in shared purpose. Here the "forgotten garden" might also reflect on the way contemporary society, and its haste, prompts us to leave our relationships untended. That the lost thing is a wallet is significant, since it could reasonably stand in for the human worlds of identity documents, commerce, and by extension the effects of humans on the landscape.

The blurb describes the book as "a fresh take on nature poetry" in the lineage of Wordsworth and Hughes. While there are compelling examples from the book that seem to bear this out, it's clear that there is more going on here than a 'retuning' of past modes. In the poems interrogating parenthood, in particular, Watts is also calling the idea of a supposed natural order of things – often invoked in arguments for static gender roles – into question.

So, while Watts favours a poetic voice that seems indirect in its engagement with the political climate when compared to the kind of work McFarlane and Sinclair are doing, there is much to celebrate in this book and in the fact of these three very different poets having released books in the same period. If the three books reviewed here are anything to go by, then there is much to look forward to in the coming year. There could be no better measure of the health of an art form than the possibility for a variety of projects and aesthetics to coexist.

Kayombo Chingonyi is the author of Some Bright Elegance *(Salt, 2012),* The Colour of James Brown's Scream *(Akashic, 2016), and* Kumukanda *(Chatto, 2017).*

ROUGH WATER, CLEAR SKIES

Eleanor Hooker, A Tug of Blue, *Dedalus, £9.95,*
ISBN 9781910251225
Philip Gross, Love Songs of Carbon, *Bloodaxe, £9.95,*
ISBN 9781780372587
Alison Brackenbury, Skies, *Carcanet, £9.99,*
ISBN 9781784101800

Jonathan Davidson considers the art of storytelling in three
new poetry collections

. . .

I n the poem 'Ablution', midway through her collection, *A Tug of Blue*,
Eleanor Hooker offers this statement:

> On my father's side
> I am part fish.
> When I am dead,
> return me to water.

And then, to balance:

> That part of me
> which is raven, on

my mother's side,
will submit.

Whether or not this is an autobiographical poem, she is certainly a poet of several parts, one being her role as helm for the Lough Derg RNLI Lifeboat. This feels significant, as Hooker's poetry flourishes at the intersection between the natural and human worlds, especially within the ecosystem of Lough Derg, with its fish and its ravens.

The collection opens with rain: "I keep my appointment with Rain" ('Weathering'). And a little later on, in 'To Stay Going',

> Rain fell like a punishment there.
> It lashed his stooped back
> when he footed turf, while ravens,
> black as guilt, jabbered at him.

While the rain may be an actor, it serves also to set the scene for the poet as fireside storyteller. So, in 'To Stay Going', a man's life is recalled in thirty-one lines, closing with a deadpan revelation:

> They say ravens ringed the chimney crown with blackthorn
> sticks, say they caught and set the thatch. Others say
> difference makes stupid men afraid, enough to douse
> bulrushes and touch the roof while he slept.

Ravens, occasionally crows, and now and then other flighted creatures, arch their baleful wings in many of Hooker's poems, although occasionally they risk too overtly signalling the darkness of the stories ahead.

The Lough (often "the lake") also gives and receives stories and features plentifully. In 'The Shout', we are given a frame-by-frame account of a lifeboat in action, and gripping stuff it is too. One of the most striking poems in the collection, 'Skipping Stones', responds to a rare moment of watery calm, while also giving the collection its title: "A rare day and the lake is a tug of blue". Reflective rather than dramatic, it offers a balance to the more self-aware poems, which can occasionally in their effort to seem demotic sound mannered. An elegy for Seamus Heaney is also quietly given, and although deeply personal offers a genuinely universal appreciation of a fellow poet, and it lifts off the page well in private recitation with some accomplished choices of line endings. As with the best poems in this collection, it finds its centre beyond the story.

In his collection *Love Songs of Carbon*, Philip Gross tells no less a story than that of the body and its inevitable change and decay. The second poem, 'This body', both signals the impact of physical decline –

> that winces sometimes
> from the mere jolt of itself (joints thickening,
> stiff gristle, nerve-ends bared)

and hints at redeeming qualities –

> See our two (do we even
>
> own them?) bodies sense each other,
> waking in the dark

Gross's desire to identify momentary pleasures is constantly challenged by his fascination with seeing just how far he can push an idea until it opens up. In 'Mould Music' his tongue-in-cheek title does not prepare us for a poem that explores how mould works its magic. He is a careful observer:

> In the moist, the dark room,
>
> the ghostly blue-grey
>
> of the lustre on the plum skin
> is developing its imprint
>
> of the after-life.

How sweetly it sounds in the mouth when read aloud adds to the potency of a poem that reminds us that our own bodies are alive with the stuff.

Gross is equally adept at considering the actions of the wider world. In the poem 'Storm Surge' he is fascinated with the power of the sea ("how a twenty-mile-wide swell / comes unpicking the seam of itself") and in 'Fission' he offers an infographic of a man diving into a sea-pool at a location called Forty Foot. This particular poem finds Gross working away at ideas to arrive at accuracy. The man entering the pool is "a quick Velcro rip" and in his descent he has shed "like a shuttle launcher [...] / [...] its umbilical cables", and finally the whole experience is "traced / in the Forty Foot collider". Another poet would have settled for less precise metaphors. The poem is made more immediate by the specificity of the location, and a number of other poems reflect Gross's Cornish origins, either placing themselves in particular locations or simply with the sea pounding away from all quarters. While Gross is not a poet of place per se, he is a relentless observer of his place in the world, of the place of human beings generally.

Alison Brackenbury is also a relentless observer, just as keen to get stuck in. 'Honeycomb', the opening poem in *Skies*, has a Keatsian appetite for sensation:

> I wonder if I live too long
>
> but then I taste the honeycomb,
> its waxen white upon my teeth,
> its liquid sun which hides beneath.

It finishes with a characteristic reality check:

> [...] In my shabby room
> I am a god. I lick the spoon.

That capacity for self-deprecation is a joy. Although she ranges over many subjects and with authority, she seems to be never far from simply voicing the experiences and responses of her readers.

This seemingly effortless accessibility does not, of course, come without effort. Brackenbury is good at managing the music of language, to the point where the challenge becomes to go back over a poem to work out just why it is so effective. The poem 'Crops', for instance, manages to eulogise the broad bean partly through offering us phrases like: "This my great-aunt took / to munch from rows, threw torn, raw green / into her morning porridge bowl." It reads well but sounds even better.

Indeed it is only by reading these poems aloud that Brackenbury's deft use of rhyme can be appreciated. In the shorter poems – some only couplets – rhyme is used to draw attention to itself to heighten the pathos, as in 'After Catullus': "I hate. I love. 'How can this be–?' you start. / I do not know. But I am torn apart." In longer poems more complicated rhyme schemes are at play, for instance in 'The Horse's Mouth', knitting together the narrative, and presumably providing the necessary syntactical challenge for creativity to flourish.

That much of this skill is not immediately apparent is perhaps because Brackenbury has some very sharp things to say, often triggered by something that would otherwise be nothing more than a modest anecdote. In 'For the New Year', a woman's feelings at receiving a "sudden gift / after thirty years" from, we assume, an old flame, triggers a self-sermon on counting one's blessings: "It was good (she told herself) not to be young, / not to bear that unending sadness, hope." The placing of sadness and hope only a comma apart is perfect, devastating. And the final line has a stage-direction that ensures that this is not a poem that offers an easy conclusion: "She stowed the gift. She kept the envelope."

Other stories are further from (apparent) personal experience but just as compelling. 'Vesta Tilley' is both a celebration of the music-hall star and First World War recruiter and also a reminder of the horrors ahead for those who responded to her call. Brackenbury's poems about Edward Thomas, Dickens and the geologist William Smith are equally fresh and revealing, treating these historical figures with the same honest compassion as more personal material. Brackenbury is a poet of strong feeling, deeply involved with her subject matter. That the work is cast with such craft and needs to do so little to draw attention to itself makes it all the more pleasurable.

Jonathan Davidson's pamphlet Humfrey Coningsby *was published by Valley Press in 2015. He is Chief Executive of Writing West Midlands.*

KALEIDOSCOPIC SECRETS

Rachael Boast, Void Studies, *Picador*, £9.99, ISBN 9781509811458
MacGillivray, The Nine of Diamonds: Surroial Mordantless,
Bloodaxe, £9.95, ISBN 9781780373249

Sophie Mayer investigates emptiness and overflow in two new
collections

. . .

Climbing over the gate into a garden
for residents only or so it says

being the perfect place to notice
a green thought gaining ground

(Rachael Boast, 'Reverdie')

Both Rachael Boast and MacGillivray (the Highland name of writer,
artist and musician Kirsten Norrie) climb over the gate into the
garden of the male poetic canon in their new collections. With different
intentions and outcomes, they each take up forms and projects generated,
if not completed, by previous experimental poets – Arthur Rimbaud and
hints of Scotland in Surrealism respectively – as "the perfect place to notice
/ a green thought gaining ground" in the development of their own poetics.

Boast's reference to Andrew Marvell's "green thought" ('The Garden') in 'Reverdie', an early poem in the cycle that comprises *Void Studies*, is as telling as her invocation of Rimbaud: these poems are as much, if not more, distinctively acknowledging a debt to the English Metaphysical-via-T.S. Eliot lineage as they are to the French Symbolists. 'A Second Time', the collection's second poem, opens:

> Time stops where the vision
> left off and the miracles began
>
> the freak fall of snow
> storm that opened the inner door

This lightly haunted house, where wind blows from front door to back, echoes Eliot's "Footfalls [...] / Down the passage which we did not take / Towards the door we never opened" ('Burnt Norton'). In Boast's collection, houses with gardens replace the electrifying cityscapes of Rimbaud's investigation of modernity and the anonymity it enables. Here, the poet walks a "bridle path" that "becomes the spine // of a well-thumbed volume / written by no-one" ('Anonymous').

The collection's closing notes intimate faintly why Rimbaud sought anonymity in the city, by quoting a comment from Paul Verlaine about his fellow poet's unrealised project, *Études néants* – from which Boast's collection takes its name. Verlaine was the teenage Rimbaud's lover, and dates Rimbaud's invention of '*néantes*' to the beginning of their relationship, suggesting that the *Études néants* may have been poems Rimbaud wrote (and destroyed) that describe their love as null. Disguised by its dominant use of second-person address, *Void Studies* nullifies the queerness of its referents: as well as Rimbaud, Boast flags Jean Cocteau ('Night of Echoes'; 'Fairytale') and Sappho ('From the French'), yet where desire is gendered, it is both explicitly ('Ranchera') and implicitly ('The Other Woman') heterosexual.

For all its traversing of the "dark which is / a harmonica" ('Eleventh Hour') there is no sense of risk in *Void Studies*, none of Rimbaud's own flinging himself at the limits. Night is kept safe – harmonious, even – by the night porter, in the poem of the same name, who

> unburdens the faces

> of the afterhours emerging from parks
> and tapas bars and relieves them
>
> until in a second their derangement
> which had become so critical evaporates

Derangement (a particularly Rimbaudian concept) is cut short by the scientism of "critical evaporates", a prescription cold shower for those who have been riskily eating tapas. Evaporation, "self-emptying" and other forms of nullification are everywhere, summed up as "again I felt myself vanishing" ('Another hive'). The quest for the void here is not hedonistic, erotic and narcotic, as it was for Rimbaud or Baudelaire, but a drowsy numbness available over-the-counter as the speaker touches willow leaves to "make aspirin" ('You tried the door'), an analgesic that cancels rather than engenders feeling.

Read against the grain, *Void Studies* could just about be a 'feminine mystique' poetics, renewing Betty Friedan's enquiry into why so many (straight white middle-class) women who appeared to 'have it all' were disaffected to the point of preferring chemical numbness. But that is to insert analysis where the poems prefer mystification, in which a torch beam is

> shining out of the need not so much
> for making sense of things as for the sense
>
> made to originate from a requisite trance
>   ('Human Torch')

A trance is indeed required to make sense of the "self-emptying" work here, whose pedestrian rhythms and vocabulary offer little in the way of narcotic, ecstatic incitement to reach that state.

By contrast, MacGillivray's *Nine of Diamonds: Surroial Mordaunt* contains all the instructions for achieving the ancient Scots practice of *taghairm*, or divination by ritual trance behind a waterfall. "[S]altire in fire / gags the derangement mouth" ('Pace 1: I') from the opening page, and the Scots derangement runs through. Scots words for plants and colours, such as 'dule', 'lyant' and 'schadow', interrupt assumed English linguistic dominance. Dominant histories are rewritten to highlight English brutality at the 1746 battle of Culloden. The titular nine of diamonds refers to a note written before the battle by the Duke of Cumberland, and the book has nine 'paces' (rather than sections or chapters), referring to the distance between the execution and executioners' blocks set up in the Old High Church Inverness, and each named for an invented suit of cards whose titles draw on Scottish mythology and scientific history. The book intertwines the work of historical recovery with the poetics of chance intuited from the form of the card game.

In doing so, MacGillivray recuperates a fellow canon-disrupter in Ossian ('James Macpherson'), suggesting that the Scots, oppressed by the English, have need of a counter-historical poetics.

As a key to all Scots mythologies, *Nine of Diamonds* works best in moments and threads, particularly where the poet's keen ear as a musician translates to the page. "[D]arkling sedge / bloom[s]" ('Pace 1: II') a Romantic wildness from the start. Where *Void Studies* aims for emptiness, *Nine of Diamonds* overflows, encompassing the Scots literary tradition, Mallarmé's *L'après-midi d'un faune*, and the *Dictionary of Phrase and Fable*. Its project is nothing less than a Scots modernist epic poem, an attempt to encapsulate Scots traditions, language and politics as Federico García Lorca did for Andalusia. Lorca is audible in the music and symbolic movement of lines such as "Lunar conquistador, moon-froth of river foam" ('Pace 4: VI').

Applying this effusive Modernism to the national mourning and cultural losses of Culloden is one thing, allowing the poet to access the "chipped [...] kaleidoscopic secret" ('Pace 9: VIV [sic]') of an obscured Scottish history. Read, however, in the context of the poet's travels across Scotland in advance of the independence referendum, the confluence of nationalism and primitivism is more problematic, highlighted by the poem's references to Egypt that derive from "the age old myth of the Highlanders as a lost tribe of Israel" ('Postscript'). 'Pace 2', repeating the invocation "– o Nile –", renders Egypt a hieroglyph of itself, which may work for HD's classicist epic *Helen in Egypt* (1961) but less so for a twenty-first-century poem attentively demanding Scotland's place in history.

Self-aware flashes of contemporaneity puncture the breathlessly hieratic evocations, calling out "a cluster-fuck of crucified fawns" ('Pace 3: VII'); more such "anti-conjuring" ('Pace 9: III') would be welcome. The prose notes make some of the best reading in the collection, particularly the long endnote on 'Pace 8' about the Gaelic visual spectrum, and the headnote to 'Pace 9', which describes the Old High Church in Culloden where executions were carried out after the battle:

Two stones can be seen, near the west door, one with two curved hollows and the other with a V-shaped groove. They are nine paces apart and in direct line. It is thought that the prisoner, blindfolded, sat on the one, or stood or knelt behind it, while the musket of the executioner rested in the groove of the other.

The colonial violence of Culloden is most viscerally present in these more documentary sections that make clear the material densely layered in the poems, almost to the point of overwhelming them.

As the poet notes in closing:

> blood makes me the ghost
> of my own slightly
> moving form – frozen blood
> dissuades my materialism.
>
> ('Pace 9: VIII')

This is not the self-erasure of *Void Studies*; the brutality of English colonial history can dissuade one's materialism – and yet, when *Nine of Diamonds* works, its "hard-rooted tongue" ('Pace 4: 5') has the measure of its urgency and complexity, particularly where it conjures the voice that speaks blazingly against erasure and into the historical and material.

> And they sing, but it's more a kind of coagulation
>
> a rising note of perished firing –
>
> a fire tone of back tense;
> pearlescent cindery bead, an own voice for stoning angels
>
> ('Pace 2: VIV [sic]')

It's such specific, physical music that is needed, in both books, to fill the void.

Sophie Mayer's most recent poetry collections are (O) (Arc, 2015) and kaolin, or How Does a Girl Like You Get to Be a Girl Like You *(Lark Books, 2015).*

ONE TO ANOTHER

Derek Walcott and Peter Doig, Morning, Paramin, *Faber, £22,*
ISBN 9780374213428
Kwame Dawes and John Kinsella, Speak from Here to There:
Two Poem Cycles, *Peepal Tree, £9.99,* ISBN 9781845233198

Karen McCarthy Woolf on the rich exchanges in two
collaborative collections

. . .

All poetry is a form of conversation: with a cloud, a flower, the
landscape, the world, the self. These two dual-authored collections
are dialogic, one taking place between poet and painter, the other poet
to poet.

Morning, Paramin is an exquisite, if formally conventional artefact, and
its layout is consistent: painting, poem, painting, poem, with the poems
predominantly taking their titles from the artworks, echoing a tradition
of call and response. Walcott explores this process as well as the images,
alongside the relationship between visual art and writing, as distinct yet
connected practices, more perhaps as in-laws than cousins. "Drawing is a
sort of duplicity", he writes in 'Figure in Mountain Landscape' – a painting
of an artist sketching – where the blurred edges of a human wearing a
peaked hood resemble and coalesce with the terrain, the human acting
as bridge between background and foreground.

Doubling emerges elsewhere, along with colour, as motif and analogy, as in for example '100 Years Ago (Carrera)', which Doig dates to 2001:

> The canoe is a hyphen between centuries,
> between generations, between trees.

This closing couplet (which, incidentally, follows an em dash) encapsulates the ekphrastic endeavour with admirable brevity: simultaneously incorporating visual representation with metaphorical extrapolation in a short, mimetic sweep.

The canoe is an emblem of precolonial island cultures and both Doig and Walcott are resident in the Caribbean: Walcott in his native St Lucia and Doig in Trinidad. Both have amplified and expanded the ways in which the postcolonial landscape is portrayed in a modern context and Walcott's legacy is one that has enriched the language and discourse through which the reader might embrace the region's history and resilience as a hybridised environment. In 'Moruga', the village Columbus is said to have sighted on Discovery Day,

> Everything has been thoroughly rehearsed.
> Doig paints it for what it is: a fable.
> Columbus never set foot here, but what is
> important is the fact that the cross-tree took root
> and spread from here its vile or virtuous practice.

One of the more mystical experiences of my life was seeing the Blue Devils descend from the mountain mist at dusk in Paramin, the king shackled to an imp and dressed as an S&M gimp. This was carnival masquerade at its most profound and its most figurative: where the intersections between African religious rite, Christianity, folklore and a choreographed improvisation of the psychosexual and cultural violence of slavery and rebellion mingle and fuse. Although this is the pairing from which the collection takes its title, the painting and the poem themselves are untitled – and conversely Walcott characterises "our island's heredity as night", not as the white marble "amputations of De Chirico" in what amounts to an aesthetic critique of a dichotomous Western canon.

No societal depiction of the West Indies – and I use this term in context – could be complete without cricket. "O the lovely vehemence of that right arm!" Walcott exclaims in 'Paragon'. Humour has its place in other poems too, as in 'Metropolitain', a celebration of intoxication. Here the speaker finds himself "in a circle of stones in a post-colonial / epoch" – a place where "to be drunk with an accent, *c'est meilleur*", (a phrase that conveniently provides a neat half-rhyme with "Baudelaire").

Later in the book there is a shift towards a more intimate, epistolary note, appropriate to the friendship between the two men, as in 'Santa Cruz II':

> [...] what the road allows is
> Trinidadian in every feature:
> murderous traffic, may you use
> great love and care with your own daughters, Peter.

White Egrets is in part an ecological mapping of St Lucia and this strand of Walcott's politics endures. In the eight lines of 'Pelican Island' we learn from Robert Devaux, "a lovely man who loved the island", that all the pelicans have been wiped out by insecticides. As the aphoristic closure of the ensuing poem 'Pelican Man' concludes:

> We have done things to nature in our time.
> The victim may be missing, but not the crime.

· · ·

Environmental activism has long been a trademark of John Kinsella whose collaboration with the Jamaican-Ghanaian poet Kwame Dawes *Speak from Here to There: Two Poem Cycles* boomerangs cross-continent from Western Australia to Nebraska where Dawes is the Chancellor's Professor of English at the university.

This is an exchange rich in contrasts and parallels: "the snow falling on your day counterpoints the ash / of burnt offerings that has coated the denials of here" writes Kinsella, from "the dead of summer" ('9'), a pronouncement that propels Dawes away from the biting Midwestern winter back to the Caribbean via the Kingston of his native Jamaica and Kamau Brathwaite's "shady backyard in Barbados" ('10'). When Dawes writes of "the petty politics / of race in civil universities" and a "small Indian woman", who is "deported by this monstrous machine", Kinsella responds with the "stress in renewing a visa so one can regain entry into / the country where my son was born". Throughout the cycle's correspondence, and as one would expect of two politically attentive poets, the daily antagonisms of aggressive global neoliberal capitalism, bigotry and the colonial inheritance are documented, ruminated and shared, via historical and contemporary literatures, music, history and personal accounts.

There are many autobiographical confidences in the poems, a trope typical to the epistle. The letter poem is a form that elicits both the immediacy of direct address and a certain intimate meandering that captures the quotidian alongside the seemingly obscure in terms of subject and thematic field. Kinsella's partner of twenty-two years, Tracy, is admitted to hospital, while Dawes writes frankly of his twenty-five-year marriage with Lorna. News of the suicide of a family friend underscores a contemplation of hereditary blindness for Dawes; Kinsella's response includes a memory of pawning the *Complete Oxford English Dictionary* at Cash Converters while he was an addict, grateful that the broker "turned a blind eye" ('63') and gave him a decent price. Both poets are rigorous in their processing of the self, its literary renditions and relationship to the locale, although unlike a posthumously published correspondence, this is not a belated exposure of privacy; the poems are aware of their future in the public domain, although they wear this prescience lightly enough. If anything, it provokes a sense of responsibility, in terms of how material is presented and processed.

At one point both poets interrogate masculinity, the trajectory of Kinsella's remembered account of his "addictions raging" alongside the relationship both men have with their fathers, their children, families and each other. The privileges of gender are all examined under the microscope of poetics, as are the pressures and fissures of racial violence as it erupts across America and Australia. An excavation of the inner emotional landscape is set against a broader, philosophical and psychoanalytic backdrop: "[...] That's the failure of twentieth- / century-and-after explorations of subjectivity, those excuses / to look into the self without responsibility, a kind of displacement", Kinsella declares.

Formally, the poem cycles shift between couplets, tercets, paragraphed verses and longer lineated blocks. While some sort of uniformity followed by each might have made it easier for the reader to instantly identify the speaker, these variations privilege the voice, and the moment, so that each poem holds as an individual entity. All are lineated, and all work within the structural paradigms of poetry as opposed to prose. At times, one poet will pick up on a comet-tail of an idea, subject or metaphorical thread and weave it into the reply, riffing off the piece that precedes it, not unlike the echoes and repetitions of the sonnet corona.

Like Walcott, who as the (not uncontested) literary monarch of the Caribbean is never far from the peripheries of Dawes's vision, Dawes initiates a consideration of the particularities of ageing, mortality and its attendant disillusions, aches and desires – both physical and emotional. This is a narrative strand that Dawes and Kinsella, being contemporaries, develop throughout. Yet there is a warmth and a reassurance too, in the correspondence itself, between a black man almost but not quite marooned in the white of America's Midwest, and a white man negotiating his own exile from the vast physical and historical dissonance of Western Australia, that builds towards a sense of urgency:

> And this is why I read your anguish
> at the brutality of then tearing apart now,
> the falsehoods of allotting to history
> what we suppose, what we conclude [...]
> This is why I have no nation, Kwame.
> ('124')

This written by Kinsella, who receives the following response:

> "This rass country woulda rass
> to hell!" This is how an ancient
> warrior breaks into a new wisdom,
> the muscle of his supreme compassion,
> despite the amassed dead [...]
> ('125')

But there is, in the end, a salve, as the book and its chronologies provoke an inevitable closure: "This is a kind of comfort, too", says Dawes, "friendship / and its persistence in memory and art, not so?" ('125'), ending on the letter's eternal syntactic invitation, the question mark.

Karen McCarthy Woolf's collection Seasonal Disturbances *is forthcoming from Carcanet this year.*

Perspective

THE SHAPE OF THE PROBLEM

Joanne Limburg asks what it means to write as an
autistic subject

I t was Induction Day for the new undergraduates at the women's
college and I was to provide part of the induction, in the form of a
talk on essay-writing technique.[1] It was an induction day for me too, the
first in my new post as Writing Fellow for this and two other colleges.
Before my talk there was lunch, an opportunity to meet the teaching staff,
and to introduce myself.

As it turned out, the Director of Studies in English and I had already
met. She asked me if I had any books in the pipeline and I told her that I
would be publishing a new collection of poetry the next year. It would be
called *The Autistic Alice*.[2] I explained that 'Alice'[3] was a vehicle for exploring

1. *I was to talk about the importance of 'killing the white', of beginning
somewhere. Some of us, I would explain, write 'generatively' – we don't
know what we think till we see what we say. I find it hard to start. But
starting at the induction seems appropriate.*
2. *This is an allusion to one of my favourite books,* The Annotated Alice,
which contains the text of Lewis Carroll's two classics, along with

my own experience,[4] and that I planned to explore it[5,6] further, in prose.

annotations in the left-hand margin of the even pages, and the right-hand margin of the odds, which Martin Gardner uses to explore the biographical, scientific, logical, satirical, literary and other allusions that pepper Carroll's work, as well as the various discussions, artworks and controversies that have arisen from it. It's a book of diversions. I love diversions.

3. By which I mean the 'Alice' in my poems, who is an autobiographical figure, a persona described in the third person; the character 'Alice' in Carroll's work; 'Alice' as used to refer to the body of work by Carroll in which the character 'Alice' appears; Martin Gardner's 'Alice'. 'Alice' here is less a portmanteau of a work, and more of a matryoshka doll. There are Alices within Alices, a mise en abyme of Alices, an infinite regression – Carroll would love that, though it is the kind of perplexity that might make his Alice cry. I love it and I want to cry.

4. The 'experience' referred to here is that of growing up with undiagnosed Asperger's Syndrome. I appreciate that the sentence with which I began this footnote is problematic in many ways. Let me lay them out for you – well, for myself and for you. First of all, is the person who had the experience the same as the person in the present who is writing about it now? As Uta Frith did not define the concept of Asperger's Syndrome until the 1980s, the concept was not widely understood until the 1990s, while I was born in 1970; could I have grown up with something that effectively did not exist as a category? Or was I just 'weird', 'awkward', 'precocious' and 'difficult to get on with'? And can I have Asperger's Syndrome now, after the American Psychiatric Association has deleted it from DSM-5 and absorbed those to whom it applies into the broader diagnosis of 'Autistic Spectrum Disorder'? Can I really have Asperger's Syndrome when I'm an adult, female, married, a mother, a teacher, a writer, not all that numerate, not all that technically minded, not terribly interested in science fiction, make eye contact, have (I hope) empathy, tell white lies, have (slowly) acquired a modicum of social and relational understanding without attending special sessions by persons specially trained to deal with persons like me and have a habit of being present in spaces where people like me are assumed not to be present? I was diagnosed at forty-two: did I have the condition before it was officially pinned to me?

5. 'My experience', I mean. I'm concerned that there's a dangling modifier here. I am concerned that a) I am not making myself clear – I can never be sure, what with my difficulties with social communication, that I am making

"I've been wondering what it would mean to write from the perspective of an autistic subject," I said.[7,8]

myself clear. Sometimes I think I am conveying the information that I am afraid, in pain, or angry, but my voice and my face let me down. I know this is writing, but what if my manner of expression here, too, is letting me down? What if it has always let me down and I have never realised? What if the written word is not after all the salvation that I have always hoped it would be? I have lived all my life in translation.

6. The other thing that concerns me about this possible dangling modifier is that it would constitute an error and I find it hard to forgive myself for making those. I find even the possibility that I will make errors an inhibiting prospect as I prepare to write, speak or otherwise interact.

7. Do I have the right to speak from this perspective? There are so many potential pitfalls. Obviously, I can only ever write from my own perspective, and I would never claim (see footnote 4) that my experience was typical or representative of that of anyone else with Asperger's Syndrome or Autistic Spectrum Disorder. My experience (my experience – hah!) of reading work by other people with the condition has been marked often by a disconcerting sense that if what they are describing is autism, then I cannot have it: I do not, for example, have any problem with metaphor – in fact, I feel very at home in it (see what I did there?). There is an expression, 'If you've met one person with autism, then you've met one person with autism'. When you get to the end of this essay, you will have read an essay about one person's autism.

8. Until fairly recently, ours (ours?) was not a subject-position from which autism was usually considered. The concept was developed and defined by clinicians. When we appeared in discourse, we did so as case studies. Autism has been defined almost exclusively by what is apparent to those who do not have it. Thus, an autistic person has been one who exhibits certain characteristics: deficits (always deficits) in social communication, semantics and pragmatics, social interaction and social imagination; limited interests; repetitive behaviours. As Steve Silberman has explained in his book NeuroTribes: The Legacy of Autism and How to Think Smarter About People Who Think Differently *(2015), parents fighting for better provision for their kids (and who had themselves had the distressing experience of being blamed for their child's condition) took up the narrative. There is plenty to read, positive, negative, or matter-of-fact, about what it is like to parent a child (almost always a child) with the condition: the sleeplessness, the disruption to family life, the distress of*

"But weren't you always writing from that perspective?" she asked.[9,10]

having a child who shows little sign of loving you back, the struggle with verbal and other learning difficulties, the frustrations and humiliations of delayed or absent toilet-training, the violent outbursts, the vicarious pain of seeing one's child ostracised, mocked or bullied by others, the wish (in some cases) that they had never been born, that they would be taken away, that they were dead. Parents who kill their disabled children are treated sympathetically, on the whole. When I write as a person with autism, I am afraid of how my writing might appear to these parents, and of how they might react: any assertion online of anything but the negative side of autism is often met by outrage and hostility from parents who are (understandably, in my view) worn out by their efforts to care and advocate for their autistic children. I would hope that our perspectives could be seen as complementary, not as contradictory. I am not saying that I understand your child better than you do. I am not saying that we are not difficult to live with or to bring up – it is distressing indeed to have to own it, but we are. I am. I am difficult to know. I caused my parents, my brother and my extended family much pain. That I never meant to doesn't stop me wanting to cry as I write this. They all died before I was diagnosed. I never got to explain. But I do know. I know.

9. See footnotes 4, 5 and 7. I replied that although, yes, by definition (arguably), I had always written from an autistic perspective, I had not done so consciously. I wanted to explore what it would mean to do so consciously. What would it mean to speak of autism in the first person singular? In the first person plural? If I can no longer say 'we' as a non-autistic person, who comes with me when I say 'we'? And how far back in history can 'we' extend? It is an uncomfortable feeling, when one's people have no roots. In response to 'queer theory', I would like to propose a 'weird theory' which enables one to read culture, present and historical, from the marginal perspective of autism. Using weird theory, we could claim Lewis Carroll and Martin Gardner's books as 'weird texts'. If I could not be a child with Asperger's in the 1970s, then Carroll could certainly not be called 'autistic' in the 1860s. However, that has not stopped autistic people from claiming him as one of their (our!) own. His biography reveals a socially awkward stammerer, with unusual and obsessive interests, a gift for logic (which I found, much to my disappointment as a philosophy student, that I do not share) and a liking for the company of children. I do not believe this had anything to do with paedophilia – as many people on the spectrum will tell you, children are often easier to get on with than non-autistic adults, with their complicated, treacherous social codes. As for the 'Alice' of the Alice books, she could be seen (as some have) as an autistic child with a logical approach to life and a tenacious insistence on what is right and appropriate, who must navigate an unpredictable and capricious neurotypical world. I identified with her from an early age (curiouser and curiouser!), and my mother always said I was like her: curious, constantly questioning and something of a "little madam". There was something about John Tenniel's pictures of Alice, too, that I identified with: she did not smile, but she gazed, levelly, and so did I. ("Smile," my teacher said to me when I was six or seven (Alice's age) with some exasperation, "You won't crack your jaw!" This was the teacher who, on another occasion when I had not intended to be naughty, called me, in front of the whole class, "A perfect pest"). (Though it was the headmaster of the junior school who told my mother I was "an average-intelligence child with a personality problem". For those who hesitate to 'label' their children, I would say this: they are going to get labelled anyway – would you rather leave it to the amateurs?).

10. And so we come (at last – thank you for your patience, I know I do go on) to the title of the essay, 'The Shape of the Problem', the problem being, in this case: What would it mean to write from an autistic perspective? When I first began to suspect that I had Asperger's Syndrome, I read a book by Julie Brown called Writers on the Spectrum: How Autism and Asperger Syndrome Have Influenced Literary Writing *(2010), in which she considered the work of various writers – Carroll included, obviously – whose biographies and oeuvres she believed to be consistent with a diagnosis of autistic spectrum disorder. She identified various features in their writing: serial structures rather than plot; diversions into areas of interest (think of Melville's whales); use of collage, pastiche, quotation and allusion – a feature she sees as akin to the echolalic aspects of autistic speech; a tendency towards autobiography; the tendency towards the exhaustive description of setting (I don't have that one). When I think about my own relation to language and to writing in particular, I notice two things. Firstly (see note 5) my reliance on it as an alternative to spoken language, which so often lets me down (or maybe it is that I let spoken language down). When I sit and write I have the leisure to explain myself, without having to monitor my interlocutor's facial expression as I do it (to try and pick up my mistakes in tone, register, body language etc), (although, see note 8 – if I write for any reader but myself I cannot do so free of social anxiety). I used to have a fantasy in early adolescence that I could give up speech altogether, in favour of explaining myself through writing: I could exercise so much more control that way, over my own expression and, to some extent, over other people's reactions too. But then there's the second thing. Freud said that a piece of language has two aspects: it is both a word presentation – a semantic thing, that means something, a unit of pragmatic exchange – and a thing presentation – an object in itself, a physical thing made of shapes on the page and sounds in the air. With this in mind, I hope you might understand what I mean if I say that I engage with language on a non-verbal level. Words for me can have meaning like a colour in a painting or a note in a song: they evoke things in me. I can sense, in a non-verbal way, inside myself, the in-itself-inarticulable shape of what I experience and what it is I mean. When I write a poem or a prose piece, I see it first as an intimation of this kind, something sensed and felt on the inside. There are some experiences that do not fit conventional rhetorical forms. If I had succeeded in making this essay compliant with them, I would have failed to convey the shape of the difficulty I was trying to articulate. It is a problem that extends not only in time but in a notional, atemporal conceptual space. And it has many wandering branches. Never mind the words. Look at the form of this piece on the page: now there is the shape of my problem.*

THE NATIONAL POETRY COMPETITION 2016

Judges: Moniza Alvi, Gerry Cambridge, Jack Underwood

The judges share comments below on the top three winners in the National Poetry Competition 2016 – Stephen Sexton, Caleb Parkin and T.L. Evans. These poems are published for the first time here. All ten winning poems can be read in the National Poetry Competition anthology and on The Poetry Society website.

Moniza Alvi on Stephen Sexton's 'The Curfew'
'The Curfew' rose to its number one position as a completely unexpected poem, a tour de force, dreamlike in its shifts, wide-ranging and deeply felt. With magic-realist leaps, it moves fluidly between a zoo's escaping animals and memories of a "legendary" miner grandfather, a very unusual man, to which the poem is, in part, an unusual tribute. The language is alive, very much the poet's own, and impressively adventurous. Take, for instance, the beauty and resonance of "the men / would mayhem bauxite by the light // his tenderness emitted". Exuberant in its energies, 'The Curfew', while scarcely pausing, admits the contemplative. It's a poem to read and reread, to ponder and to experience. Its conclusion tenders that which goes beyond accustomed language, beyond any language: "I feel under my wings // the words for things I thought I knew / departing, and I understand him."

Jack Underwood on Caleb Parkin's 'The Desktop Metaphor'
I really like the way that the form and the repetitions in this poem make for something a bit churchy, a bit call-and-response, and at the same time the way the phrases develop and mutate, layering up each assertion. By the end the poem has come full-circle, but it's not the same circle we started off with: something has been shifted. Also I love "The Great Stapler" and the "Photo Copier", which lend a humorous, imaginative tone to the grinding office job the "Gods of our Days" undertake in their administration of the "things that matter". It's weird, and smart, and confident, bringing something vast, strange and unresolvable within reach.

Gerry Cambridge on T.L. Evans's 'Detuned Radio'

'Detuned Radio' is an impeccably constructed poem with an intriguing echo of the narrator's uncle in Robert Frost's 'A Servant to Servants', kept in a cage. The child's "rage" is extreme: neither medicine nor religion, with its hint at the attempt to cure demonic possession, can affect it. The first stanza recounts the narrator's memory of him or herself as that child. The second stanza switches, more or less entirely, to the present. Only the last two lines of the poem go some way to explaining the source of the child's rage – a dead twin – and personify what had been, up till then, "the desperate presence", "the thing". 'Detuned Radio' is an oorie poem which never quite reveals its full hand. It uses the suggestiveness of subtle horror to light the reader's imagination. Its sense of pacing, the way the sentences are laid into the stanzas, with no enjambments, is beautifully handled. Its last line makes the hairs stand up on the back of my neck.

. . .

National Poetry Competition 2016 Winners

First prize:	Stephen Sexton, 'The Curfew'
Second prize:	Caleb Parkin, 'The Desktop Metaphor'
Third prize:	T.L. Evans, 'Detuned Radio'
Commended:	Marc Brightside, 'Eleven Years of May'
Commended:	Patrick James Errington, 'Never Say Never Say Never'
Commended:	Sam Harvey, 'Claire Climbs Everest'
Commended:	Fran Lock, 'Epistle from inside the Sharknado'
Commended:	Laura Scott, 'The Grey Mirror'
Commended:	Holly Singlehurst 'Hiroshima, 1961'
Commended:	Peter Wallis, 'What Can I Say?'

STEPHEN SEXTON

The Curfew

The radicals sprung the locks that night, hurrah!
and their lovely collarbones were almost moonly.

Rhinos shrieked and bellowed, elephants tromboned
and the animals nosed into town.

Sunrise to sunrise and sunrise we kept indoors.
If you can't count your onions, what can you count

my grandfather used to say. He said a lot of things.
Among the other miners he was legendary:

when no more than the thought of the pink crumple
of his infant daughter's body came to mind

a glow would swell in the pit, the men
would mayhem bauxite by the light

his tenderness emitted.
Some of me lived inside her even then.

The memorial fountain says nothing
of the weeks before the rescue failed

but mentions God which, as my grandfather
used to say, is just the name of the plateau

you view the consequences of your living from.
Or something like that. He said a lot of things.

He grew wise and weary as an albatross
and left for that great kingdom of nevertheless.

It would have pleased his handsome shoulders
to watch this grizzly scoop for salmon

in the fountain of his friends, or the Bengals,
or the shakedown squad of chimpanzees

who bang and bang on the grocery window.
One by one eleven miners starved to death.

In the streets they collar or tranquillise
the ocelots and run a spike of ketamine

through the plumbing in the fountain.
Dromedaries blue-mood around the pub

aloof under their reservoirs of fat.
I don't sleep, but oh plateau! these days

of violence have been my happiest.
Even a cabbage is not without desire

my grandfather said one day, and now
among the animals, I feel under my wings

the words for things I thought I knew
departing, and I understand him.

CALEB PARKIN

The Desktop Metaphor

there are holes in the sky
we name them
after things that matter
and the Gods of our Days
like The Great Stapler
which attaches the night to us
and the ideas to words
that are just light

and we name them
after things that matter
and the Gods of our Days
like The Great Stapler
which attaches the night to us
and the words to ideas
that are just light
packaged in dark matter

dark matter
first class to our eyes
know their names
things that matter
the Photo Copier
scanning and remembering us
we were exoplanets

sent first class to our eyes
so we might know their names
these things that matter
like the Photo Copier
scanning and remembering us
as though we were exoplanets
with atmospheres of ink

ink
mating cries
the Gull
the poles
tectonic
eyes
not matter
name them

full of bright mating cries
from Gods of our Days like the Gull
whose beak marks the poles
whose screams are tectonic
in the bin-man's crackling eyes
where names do not matter
so we name them
holes in the sky

T.L. EVANS

Detuned Radio

My mother said she'd never known such rage
within a child, she told me later,
after the doctor, and after the pastor.
I don't recall the nights within the cage.
I'd raise my two-foot frame against the bars
and fill the little room, my mother said,
with screaming, *screaming that could wake the dead,*
my fists and eyes clamped shut against the dark.
I don't remember much till I was saved.
It was by chance her detuned radio
whose crackling plugged the quiet's monstrous hole.
I sank beneath its filtered, whispered waves.

Still now, when silence starts to sink its gap,
I hear the desperate presence climbing up
and twitch the dial to static's frequency.
Its hiss alone can make the thing retreat.
We used to top and tail, me and my twin.
And when the white noise stops she speaks again.

CONTRIBUTORS

Fleur Adcock's next collection, *Hoard*, is due from Bloodaxe in October • **Gary Allen**'s most recent collections are *Jackson's Corner* (Greenwich Exchange Publishing, 2016) and *Mapland* (Clemson University Press, 2017) • **Gillian Allnutt** is the recipient of the Queen's Gold Medal for Poetry 2016. Her most recent collection is *indwelling* (Bloodaxe, 2013) • **Raymond Antrobus**'s second pamphlet, *To Sweeten Bitter*, is forthcoming from Outspoken Press. His debut collection will be published by Penned in the Margins in 2018 • **Khairani Barokka** is author-illustrator of *Indigenous Species* (Tilted Axis Press, 2016). Her full-length poetry collection *Rope* (Nine Arches Press, 2017) is forthcoming • **Jennifer Bartlett**'s most recent book is *Autobiography/Anti-Autobiography* (theenk Books, 2014). She is a co-editor of *Beauty Is a Verb: The New Poetry of Disability* (Cinco Puntos Press, 2011) • **A.K. Blakemore**'s debut poetry collection, *Humbert Summer*, was released in 2015 • **Mary Jean Chan** won the Oxford Brookes International Poetry Competition 2016 (ESL). She is a co-editor at *Oxford Poetry* • **Patrick Cotter** has been published in *London Review of Books*, *Poetry*, *PN Review* and elsewhere • **John Lee Clark** is a DeafBlind poet, essayist, and independent scholar from Minnesota. His latest book is the essay collection *Where I Stand: On the Signing Community and My DeafBlind Experience* (Handtype Press, 2014) • **Johnny Damm** is a writer specialising in verbal-visual and creative-critical blends. *Science of Things Familiar* (The Operating System, 2017) is his most recent publication • **Joe Dunthorne**'s poetry pamphlet appeared in the Faber New Poets series in 2010. His third novel, *The Adulterants*, will be published in February 2018 • **Jameson Fitzpatrick** is the author of the chapbook *Morrisroe: Erasures* (89plus/LUMA Publications). He teaches writing at New York University • **Aracelis Girmay**'s latest collection is *The Black Maria* (BOA Editions, 2016) • **Peter Gizzi**'s most recent book is *Archeophonics*; in 2018 Carcanet will bring out a *New & Selected Poems* • **Yael Hacohen** has an MFA in Poetry from New York University. She was a NYU Veterans Workshop Fellow and is Editor-in-Chief at *Nine Lines Literary Review* • **Nicola Healey** was commended in the Resurgence Poetry Prize 2015. She is the author of *Dorothy Wordsworth and Hartley Coleridge: The Poetics of Relationship* (Palgrave Macmillan, 2012) • **Rita Ann Higgins**'s most recent collection is *Tongulish* (Bloodaxe, 2016) • **Tyehimba Jess**'s first book of poems, *leadbelly*, was a winner of the 2004 National Poetry Series. His second collection is *Olio* (Wave Books, 2016) • **Sylvia Legris**'s *Nerve Squall* (Coach House Books, 2005) won the 2006 Griffin Poetry Prize. Her latest book is *The Hideous Hidden* (2016) • **Joanne Limburg**'s third collection, *The Autistic Alice*, is published by Bloodaxe this year • **Layli Long Soldier** is the author of the chapbook *Chromosomory* (2010) and the recently published *Whereas* (2017). She is a citizen of the Oglala

Lakota Nation • **John Maucere** is an actor and performer of American Sign Language poetry • **Kei Miller** won the Forward Poetry Prize in 2014 for his collection *The Cartographer Tries to Map a Way to Zion* • **Angel Nafis** is the author of *BlackGirl Mansion* (Red Beard/New School Poetics, 2012) and recipient of the 2016 Ruth Lilly and Dorothy Sargent Rosenberg Fellowship and the 2017 NEA Creative Writing fellowship • **Vi Khi Nao** is the author of *Fish in Exile* (Coffee House Press, 2016) and *The Old Philosopher* (Nightboat Books, 2016) • **Kate Potts** is currently completing a practice-based PhD on the poetic radio play • **Alison C. Rollins** was a recipient of the Ruth Lilly and Dorothy Sargent Rosenberg Poetry fellowship in 2016 • **Lucy Tunstall**'s first collection is *The Republic of the Husband* (Carcanet, 2014) • **Jan Wagner**'s most recent collection, *Regentonnentonnenvariationen* ('Rain Barrel Variations'), won the 2015 Leipzig Book Fair Award • **James Warner**'s poems have appeared occasionally in Canadian literary journals for many years • **Jennifer Wong** is the author of *Goldfish* (Chameleon Press, 2013). She is currently completing a PhD on place and identity in contemporary Chinese diaspora poetry at Oxford Brookes • **Zhou Zan** 周瓒 (also known as Zhou Yaqin) is a leading Chinese poet, translator, playwright and critic.

Permissions: Four 'Whereas Statements' © 2017 by Layli Long Soldier, from her collection *WHEREAS*, published by Graywolf Press.

the Bridport Prize
poems | short stories | flash fiction | novels

CLOSING DATE 31ST MAY 2017
Poems | 1st prize £5000
judge Lemn Sissay

Short Stories | 1st prize £5000
judge Peter Hobbs

Flash Fiction | 1st prize £1000
judge Kit De Waal

Novel Award | 1st prize £1000
judge Nathan Filer

enter online | www.bridportprize.org.uk

THE**POETRY**SOCIETY

The Poetry Society and judges Jo Bell, Bernard O'Donoghue and Kathryn Williams congratulate the following on being shortlisted for the Ted Hughes Award for New Work in Poetry 2016

Jay Bernard, *The Red and Yellow Nothing*
Will Eaves, *The Inevitable Gift Shop*
Salena Godden, *LIVEwire*
Harry Man, *Finders Keepers*
Melissa Lee-Houghton, *Sunshine*
Hollie McNish, *Nobody Told Me*
Caroline Smith, *The Immigration Handbook*

The winner of the award will be announced on 29 March 2017. For more information, visit poetrysociety.org.uk/tha

Crow by Leonard Baskin. Reproduced by kind permission of Lisa Baskin and the Estate of Leonard Baskin.

TED HUGHES AWARD FOR NEW WORK IN POETRY

LEDBURY POETRY FESTIVAL 2017
21 YEARS

POETRY COMPETITION

30 JUNE – 09 JULY

JUDGE: FIONA SAMPSON MBE

First Prize: £1000 and a residential writing course at Tŷ Newydd

Second Prize: £500

For more information and to download the entry form visit poetry-festival.co.uk/ledbury-poetry-competition/

Photo: Ekaterina Voskresenskaya

Follow us on Twitter @ledburyfest or find us on Facebook

poetry-festival.co.uk

Closing date: Thursday 13 July 2017

Canolfan Ysgrifennu Tŷ Newydd Writers' Centre

Supported using public funding by
ARTS COUNCIL ENGLAND

Connect to the power of poetry on your PC, Mac, iPhone or iPad

The Poetry Review digital

The finest poetry at your fingertips – The Poetry Review, wherever you are in the world

THE Poetry Review

Gillian Allnutt
Mary Jean Chan
Layli Long Soldier
Kei Miller
Jan Wagner

Image: bit.ly/mobilephoto1

The digital edition of *The Poetry Review* means you can browse and search the latest issue – and back issues – of the world's finest poetry magazine on your PC, Mac, iPhone and iPad, from anywhere in the world. Here's how you do it...

Add a digital subscription to your Poetry Society membership
If you receive *The Poetry Review* as part of your Full membership of The Poetry Society, then all you have to do to gain FREE access to the digital version of *The Poetry Review*, is register, using your membership number, at **exacteditions.com/print/thepoetryreview**

Free to FULL Members of The Poetry Society

Not yet a member? Add a digital subscription to your existing print subscription
Add digital access to your print subscription for just £24.99 per annum. Sign up at exacteditions.com/thepoetryreview. For details of multi-user access for colleges and universities, visit **exacteditions.com/library/thepoetryreview**

Even better – join The Poetry Society as a Full Member! For full details, visit **poetrysociety.org.uk/membership**, or contact Paul McGrane on 020 7420 9881.

THE**POETRY**SOCIETY

Supported using public funding by
**ARTS COUNCIL
ENGLAND**